Psychic Suburbia

Psychic Suburbia

By Cassandra Eason

foulsham

London•New York•Toronto

foulsham

The Publishing House, Bennetts Close,
Cippenham, Berkshire, SL1 5AP

ISBN 0-572-02036-8
Copyright © 1994 Cassandra Eason

Designed and typeset by WightWitch Editorial Services
Isle of Wight
Printed in Great Britain by St Edmundsbury Press Ltd,
Bury St Edmunds, Suffolk.

Psychic Suburbia is a book that has grown out of years of conversations with people who are not usually clairvoyants, owners of haunted stately homes, mediums or mystics — at least not to begin with.

They are people into whose life another world has intruded as they went about their ordinary, day-to-day business. Sometimes the supernatural has touched them briefly and left them bewildered but unchanged. In other cases, the paranormal has changed their lives, although not in the way you might expect.

These experiences are more common than many people would like to admit. Most families have a story to tell of some inexplicable incident. Your town, your street is Psychic Suburbia.

Cassandra Eason

Contents

Chapter One

Breaking Into The Spirit World

DAVID BRYAN WAS breaking into a shop in Hockley in Birmingham when he saw his first ghost. 'I was only a teenager and my brother and I thought it would be a laugh to climb through the window into the tobacconist's storeroom while she was asleep and steal some cigarettes. It was about 2am and we were filling a box with cigarettes. We both looked towards the main window and saw the figure of a woman in grey float towards us. We ran out of the shop as fast as we could and flew over the wall. We got such a fright that we forgot that we'd left the gate open for a quick getaway in case the police had arrived.

'Up till that point I didn't believe in ghosts or spirits or anything because it suited me not to believe so I could do just what I like. But that experience put me on the straight and narrow. Otherwise I might have ended up like a lot of my friends in and out of gaol. I am 47 years old and have never been in trouble with the law.'

Hockley, with its mix of old terrace houses and council property, corner shops and pubs, deep in the heart of inner-city Birmingham, is hardly the sort of place in which a conventional ghost tale would be set. Nor is David, a West Midlands country and western singer, the sort of character who would feature in the conventional ghost story. But this is not a conventional ghost story book of old dark houses, phantoms of the haunted wood or Transylvanian vampires. Here we are talking about Psychic Suburbia.

For the psychic world has moved on from the wild moorlands and ruined castles of ancient times for the warmer and infinitely friendlier setting of the centrally-heated front rooms in modern towns, villages, bedsits and housing estates while the wise woman has exchanged her cave in the woods for a semi in Acacia Avenue, or a booth at the end of the pier at Southend. But the psychic world today, though in more down-to-earth setting retains its old purpose: to give glimpses of another dimension and a helping hand from beyond when the going gets rough. Nowhere is this needed more than our own age, where people are driven by the pressure to possess consumer goods while recession has made even basic necessities impossible for many.

Life is hard for people today in a different way from the physical stresses suffered by our ancestors. Television adverts and soap operas put forward images of domestic bliss and the body beautiful that bear little resemblance to the mundane lives many of us live in reality. I am a housewife with five children and I'm writing this chapter in between mopping up the deluge from a leaking washing machine and getting the children's tea.

Sceptics say that those who believe in the supernatural

are looking back to a golden age that never was, when life was simpler. But the truth is more complex. For many people do not go looking for occult experiences but find they are forced upon them. Somehow, the psychic world intrudes into our safe suburban lives.

The most common occurrence is some sort of telepathy. (Who needs telepathy, say the sceptics, when you've got a telephone? Obviously their experience of British Telecom has been better than mine). Telepathy between friends and family is so commonplace that often we barely notice it. There are the little things: you and your mother often phone each other at exactly the same moment and get the engaged tone. Or you know when your grown-up son at the other end of the country is in trouble. But doesn't everybody? Yes, and that's what makes the psychic so exciting. Most of us use psychic abilities without realising.

I found a fascinating case of telepathy in the archives of the Alister Hardy Research Centre in Oxford. James who lives in Chelmsford, in Essex, wrote: 'Eight times out of 10, my wife can know when her mother is going to phone or write though there is no pattern. Her brothers are much closer to the mother but they can't do it. One day about 10am the phone rang and I said, "I wonder who it is?"

' "Oh, it's Susan phoning from Heathrow Airport," my wife replied.

'Susan was our bridesmaid of 20 years before and we hadn't seen her for years as she was living in Nairobi. But it was Susan on the phone from Heathrow. She hadn't told my wife but there had been problems in her marriage and she'd suddenly decided to fly back to England and was going to surprise us. I was certainly surprised.'

Predictive powers too are very common and can some-

11

times give us a chance to panic in advance. So when the crunch comes we are ready to cope. Amy, who lives in a south coast resort, woke from a vivid dream and saw her 20-year-old son, Jim, walking down the corridor outside her room: 'He was wearing a red motor bike jacket I'd not seen before. I suddenly knew that he was going on the back of someone's motor bike and that I must warn him. I said to him, "Be careful Jim. Make sure you don't have an accident. If you go on the motor bike you'll hurt your legs". And then I realised he wasn't there at all and wasn't due home till late.

'The vision made no sense. My son had taken his car out for the evening and didn't have a motor bike or a red motor bike jacket. But the feeling wouldn't go away and I couldn't get back to sleep. I didn't know where to contact him. Besides what could I say? I'd sound like a fussy mother hen.

'At 2.10am the doorbell rang. I opened it and a policeman stood outside.

' "Jim's hurt his legs in a motor bike accident," I said without thinking.

' "Has the hospital phoned you then?" the policeman asked.

'Jim had met some friends in town and transferred to the pillion of a bike and borrowed a jacket. There had been a crash and he was in hospital having injured both legs.'

Amy's vision prepared her for the shock so she could panic in advance and be able to remain calm when the crisis came. And a positive result of premonitions can be that we are able to help our loved ones when they need us most.

Many people do have a psychic experience during their lives — few are untouched by sorrow or intense joy — and afterwards their worlds are never the same. Psychic Suburbia tells their stories and you'll know they are real because, unlike some more colourful tales of psychic adventure, the solution isn't instant and all the ends tied up. Life isn't like that and you wouldn't believe me if I told you otherwise.

Guardian angels too have moved with the times. On the moors of Devon on a dark night you might see an isolated farmhouse in the distance. You may be tempted to believe that perhaps here is a place where Brownies or Boggits might come to lend a hand with the milking or other tasks, in return for the bowl of milk which country folk would leave out for them. But move east towards the urban sprawl of Bristol and the only Brownies you would come across would be those that grow up into Girl Guides. So any helpful spirit has to take a new guise and the modern guardian angel is more likely to appear as a city gent than the more traditional winged kind. At least that is what Iris from Bristol found. She began receiving messages from a spirit guide who spoke like a retired BBC announcer — perhaps that is what he was in a previous life.

Iris had the habit of lighting a cigarette as soon as she woke. But one morning early her angel woke her up and insisted: 'Get up now.'

'I ignored him as I was tired,' said Iris, 'but he kept on and on at me. "Get up now, Iris," he kept saying.

'And so, at 6.30, I gave up trying to lie there, got up and opened the bedroom door. The house was filled with gas.'

Had Iris stayed in bed as usual and lit her early morning cigarette she might have met her angelic friend in person. Was this a paranormal health warning? Was it some subconscious awareness manifesting itself as a voice? Or was it really a kindly, cultured spirit who was anxious that

13

his protegee finished her allotted earthly span? Whatever the source, the result was entirely positive.

So this book is not about those phantoms and clairvoyants who make the headlines, but about the ordinary people who have shared their psychic experiences or searchings with me. Some stories I have discovered in archives. But many more stories come from the people I have met in the course of my everyday life — people I get talking to in the street, on trains and even in the supermarket queue. The stories are there for any sympathetic listener to uncover, homely experiences that often get missed out from more elevated surveys or formal paranormal research. Yet these are perhaps the strongest proof that life and relationships go on hereafter in ways not very different from our here and now.

Other people write to me or phone for advice because they are worried by the sudden onset of psychic phenomena into the world they believed they had the measure of. So I put down the dripping washing, or switch off the vacuum cleaner, and listen. And that is what people really want; not to fill in a form or carry out card-guessing experiments in a laboratory in order to try to demonstrate an ability that is almost always tied up with love and real relationships.

I was looking for my son's lost school bag when Stacey, who lives in High Wycombe in Buckinghamshire, phoned with a far more riveting mystery. She was worried because strange things had begun to happen since her new baby had been born two weeks before . The incidents had started when she had got back together with a former boyfriend whom she'd known in her teens. Neither set of parents had approved of the relationship, but recently Stacey had seen Colin's deceased mum and he'd seen her

14

late dad. This was all very reassuring for Stacey who felt that perhaps they had come to say they approved of the relationship reviving 12 years later. Or perhaps they had even popped in to see the new baby — it often happens that a ghostly gran or grandad comes to see a new arrival.

But the recent events were more sinister. Things were moving, photographs were being placed face down and a chain of Colin's that had the links fastened so tightly that they could only be cut off had, apparently disappeared and then appeared days later hanging on a hook in the bedroom. Stacey and Colin had felt sinister presences and Stacey's young daughter had been frightened by a girl she said was called Mary who came to talk to her in the night.

At last Colin had gone to see a medium who had quite spontaneously told him there was a child around who was behaving maliciously. Why? Stacey asked me. And it didn't seem to make sense because births usually attract benign presences.

Had it been a living child behaving badly I would have said jealousy and of course Stacey's little girl would have been a prime candidate for moving things. But most of the incidents happened while Stacey, her boyfriend and daughter were out and, indeed, were happening at Colin's unoccupied and very secure flat. So I inquired very tactfully if Stacey had lost any children. She told me that 12 years before, she had quite a late abortion when she was only 16. Her late mother-in-law had been the one who insisted Stacey gave up the child and even when Stacey had her pre-med and begged to keep her baby, the older woman insisted the abortion went ahead. Stacey said though she and her mother-in-law had made peace shortly before her death Stacey had never forgiven her deep down.

It wouldn't help to speculate whether the poltergeist was Stacey's lost daughter, or her late mum-in-law unable to rest. Nor would it help to wonder if Stacey's own regrets for her lost child, which were especially strong at this time, were creating negative psychic energy. The important thing was to restore harmony to the home. I suggested that Stacey might like to ask a priest or the president of her local Spiritualist church to perform a simple blessing ceremony to settle things down and above all if Stacey could forgive her mother in law and let her rest then the living family could move forward.

So a case of a poltergeist suddenly becomes understandable when looked at in domestic terms. After all, ghosts were once people who lived and loved and sometimes made ghastly mistakes that perhaps have haunted them beyond the grave.

We need to go back to grass roots to understand the psychic world as it touches our own. For it is all around us as we work, cook, watch television and travel — not to Tibet or the Kalahari desert for enlightenment but on the 8.22 from Woking to Waterloo. Yet the world of psychic suburbia is a hidden one. People don't readily talk about their psychic experiences over the garden wall or in the pub for fear of being thought cranky, and time after time I am asked not to use names and to change details. For real psychic experiences are intensely personal and often very precious.

What is more, at this grass roots level the trappings of the paranormal may be more mundane. Take for example what is known as a Near Death Experience. These sometimes occur when a person is badly-injured or undergoing some sort of operation which could be life-threatening and appears to 'die' for a short time. Survivors have recounted leaving their bodies and viewing the operation or the attempted rescue from outside. Then they have embarked on astral journeys, sometimes travelling to a heavenly place complete with pearly gates.

But this view of the after-life can sometimes be urbanised. Doris Dunn lives in Bracknell, a town which is fast swallowing the Berkshire countryside between it and Reading. She told me of her brush with eternity, when she was in her late sixties, as we drank coffee in the living room of her comfortable sheltered flat.

'In 1983, I was very ill with viral pneumonia and I was not expected to live. I woke up very early one morning in hospital and watched the sun rise. "Please take me over," I cried. "I'm sick of all this pain and illness."

' "No," said a voice, "you've still got work to do."

'I found myself behind a long brick wall. I decided to try to get to the end to see what was round the other side. But I was so tired. "Please give me a sign I'll get better," I prayed.

'Suddenly it was as if I was on a high hill. I thought I'd arrived at the Eternal City. But it wasn't the Eternal City I was looking at but down on Bracknell at night with all the bright lights of the Ring Road spread out before me.

'I flew across it like a bird and saw all the houses and the town centre like fairyland below. Then there was a great wind and I found myself in bed and in pain again. But from that moment I did get better and not long afterwards met Alf who had just lost his wife and before long we got married. I believe that's why I was sent back to make him happy.'

Alf beamed contentedly as Doris bustled off to get his tea.

Many of the experiences in the book occur spontaneously and usually when least expected, whether they are one-off experiences or continue over several years. And as such they can be uplifting, assuring us that there is more to life than the daily slog followed by another evening watching the telly.

For when disaster strikes, whether through accident, illness, bereavement, divorce, redundancy or simply everyday doubts and depression we do need all the help we can get. Today's throwaway society offers no real solutions or consolation. And perhaps that is the key to why the psychic plays such a vital part in ordinary people's lives. A modern street, bedsitter land or a housing estate can be a very lonely place if you've got no one when you close the curtains. Families may live miles away and perhaps be divided by divorce, remarriage or single parenthood. Community togetherness, where, in the words of a current soap opera, 'good neighbours are only a footstep away', is often more myth than reality.

So people turn to clairvoyants and mediums for a bit of good news and a friendly ear. But the whole thing can get out of hand if you are lonely or unhappy. It is tempting to pay for a bit of good news or someone to listen just for a while to your problems and maybe offer a magical solution.

Go to any psychic fair and see the people, usually women, not New Age followers or yuppies eager to find enlightenment, but ordinary wives and mothers from Surbiton, Southend or Stockport. They are queuing knee deep and exchanging money as though it were the first day of the sales, in return for promises of a brighter tomorrow, or the day after. Others may spend a fortune on postal clairvoyants or buying an expensive talisman or spells to bring back an unfaithful partner or finds a new love.

I'm not saying all clairvoyants are frauds. I know many honest decent ones who do much good. But if we hand over our future to anyone, however psychic, then we are handing over our own very real power to choose our destiny. In a later chapter I tell of the women who have exchanged hard-earned cash for promises of instant love or fortune and of the clairvoyants and mediums who live at the end of the street and dispense wisdom and healing while bemoaning the price of tea at the corner shop.

A brush with the paranormal or a clairvoyant who hints at undeveloped psychic abilities of our own, (but watch out for those who offer to develop them for a fat fee) can trigger off an active search to develop forgotten or never used psychic powers that we all possess as part of our instinctive make-up. Psychic groups can be a great source of personal as well as psychic strength and a good night out, so long as common sense is a vital component.

Such a group flourished in Reading, Berkshire. The town offers a wide range of entertainment — sports centres, cinemas, discos and pubs — but to give herself a night out with a difference, Gaynor, a mother of two children, went along to the psychic group with a friend and found she had a gift for psychometry. This is based on the theory that objects can record vibrations of events connected with their owners which a gifted psychometrist can replay like a video recorder. Sir Arthur Conan Doyle, the creator of Sherlock Holmes and an ardent spiritualist, used psychometry as the basis for a short story, *The Leather Funnel,* but I do not recommend that you read it unless you have very, very strong nerves as it is a real chiller.

Conan Doyle had his characters sleep with an object under their pillow in order that they might receive the impressions in their dreams. But Gaynor found that she could hold an object then be able to tell the owner about its past. At first she found this frightening. But the leader of her psychic group explained that it was an extension of the instinctive ability that we all have to sum up people and situations.

The power came in useful in an unexpected way. Ginny, a girl Gaynor worked with, showed her an antique ring that Ginny's new boy-friend had offered as token of their golden future together. Francis had told Ginny it was a family heirloom and had belonged to his late grandma. Gaynor held it then said automatically: 'No, he won it gambling.'

Ginny was quite miffed and Gaynor wished she'd kept her mouth shut although she felt quite strongly that Francis was involved quite heavily into gambling and there had been a dispute over the ownership. But what Gaynor said must have struck a chord with Ginny who mentioned that Francis had borrowed quite a few sums of money from her that he had not repaid.

The next morning Ginny was very subdued. Francis had asked her to lend him quite a large sum — she'd recently inherited some when her grandmother had died. Ginny had asked him if the money was for a gambling debt. He had admitted that it was and seemed surprised that she was upset about this.

Francis had assured her that it was an investment as he had been tipped off about a sure-fire winner and they could both give up work and go off to live in the sun.

I do not know if Francis's sure-fire winner did make it first past the post because their relationship broke up over the gambling issue. Gaynor felt very guilty about it because there was the outside chance that Francis could have made their fortune with his horse and he and Ginny could have been happy ever after. But in some ways the possession of a little psychic ability can be just as uncertain as the spin of a roulette wheel. You must take a chance on speaking out about what you know or keep quiet.

As for Ginny, shortly after the incident she met a new man and is relying on her own instincts in the lottery of love.

There is a dark side to psychic suburbia that too often is either sensationalised or swept under the carpet. Clergy and psychologists utter dire warnings, some with good reason, about dabbling in the occult. But to pretend that our psychic nature doesn't exist is to deny a vital and indeed spiritual part of our make-up. Psychic powers, like everything else, are subject to abuse and misuse, often with dire consequences. But there cannot be an entirely positive entity — even Christianity has its Devil. And when dark, spontaneous, psychic happenings occur, then they may be reflecting a deeper discontent with our earthly lives.

Ted, who lives in Greater Manchester, held regular seances in his front room with his wife and friends when the kids were asleep. Often the information passed on by the spirit proved useful: a small win on the horses using the tips given or a scandalous titbit from someone's past to cause hilarity at work. Ted got a reputation as a bit of a psychic and he started to think of himself as having powers. But one night a malevolent old man who said he had been a tramp who had been stabbed to death in an alley in Salford dominated the ouija board and refused to go away. When Ted ended the session, the light bulb smashed for no apparent reason.

The next day Sue, Ted's three-year-old daughter, refused to go into the front room saying there was a smelly old tramp sitting on the settee. Her parents tried to reassure her but the child persisted and would cry at night because the old man was following her. At last her father admitted to a spiritual healer that he had been regularly dabbling. The healer persuaded the spirit to leave, but it was a long time before Sue would go into the front room alone and occasionally Ted still detects the odd shadow and wonders. He's a lot less keen now on exhibiting his foreknowledge and has kept clear of ouija sessions.

So *Psychic Suburbia* is the story of the real men and women and their paranormal experiences, good and bad, who live in your road or on your estate or in the next flat. Perhaps I am telling your story or one which is similar to it. There are certainly a few of mine scattered around. As I said, magic isn't out there happening to other people. It's home and dry. Just knock at any door, or come with me and listen.

Chapter Two

The Spectral Semis

T AKE A LOOK down the terraced or semi-detached streets of neat little houses with their well-washed cars and satellite dishes and they seem safe havens of 20th-Century snugness, safe from ghoulies and ghosties and things that go bump in the night. Of course, if you travel out into the country, perhaps to one of our stately homes, it is a different story.

There, where the very walls seem to speak of days gone by, it is easy to slip back mentally to a time when our ancestors walked a little faster towards the house as dusk fell, so as to be safe indoors when the Green Man began to prowl through the woods. A time when that hound, baying in the distance, might just be Black Shuck or one of the other devil dogs whom it was death merely to see.

You can feel a delightful tingle down your spine as you mount an old oaken staircase and are told that at certain times of the year the White Lady has been seen descending it, wailing for her long dead lover; or in that room the ghost of Sir Charles, who was poisoned by his own children can be heard crying for vengeance.

Such places are meat and drink to the professional ghost hunters, who congregate in them, when they can get permission, to try to bring back positive proof of spectres. In they go, armed with elaborate cameras, electric eyes, tape recorders and all the weapons of modern science. Needless to say they fail and are surprised, just like my children who crash through the woods shouting at the tops of their voices, 'Rabbits, come on rabbits. Where are you rabbits? Show yourselves', and then report back: 'There aren't any rabbits here mummy'.

But if you are quiet and sympathetic to a place, you may catch a glimpse or a feeling of something from beyond. Imagination or something more? If you ask anyone about it, they will inform you according to their own prejudices. In many cases it is best to judge for yourselves.

But most people will tell you that this glimpse of another world will disappear when you make your way back to suburbia and the usual grind of work or family life. Or will it? Pat lives in no-nonsense Bromley in Kent. But she found her life changed when she visited Ightham Mote, near Seven Oaks, described in guide books as a charming old manor-house enclosing a court and sur-rounded by a moat.

It dates from the 14th Century but possesses a late 15th Century gate-tower and 'an admirable specimen of a Tudor domestic chapel' which dates back to around 1530. Until the last century, the house was owned by the Selby family, devout Catholics who held fast to their religion secretly during the times when it was banned. Because of this, there are extra locks on the chapel door where secret services where held in the crypt and the usual priest holes and escape routes. In other words, it is the perfect setting for a ghost story.

At the time, Pat could have done with a little escapism into the past for her present was none too bright. Her marriage was under tremendous strain.

'I went to Ightham Mote with my sister,' Pat told me. 'In one room I felt the most terrible sorrow and a strong frightening presence. There was a huge inglenook fireplace in the room and on impulse I took a piece of loose stone home as a souvenir.

'When I got up the next morning all the chairs in my dining room were tipped over and the back of my watch was smashed in. That was where I'd left the stone. Then I smelled this dreadful odour like rotting flesh, the smell you get when meat has gone right off. And then I saw her, a woman all dressed in black whose hands were torn and bleeding. "Please help me," she cried over and over again. "They shut me behind the wall though I did no wrong!" '

There is an escape route for priests behind a chimney in Ightham Mote and the skeleton of a woman was found in a cupboard behind a walled-up doorway in the tower. The body was discovered in 1872 by workmen and it is possible that the woman was Dorothy Selby, a cousin of Lord Monteagle. An anonymous letter to Lord Monteagle, warning him not to go to Parliament on November 5th, 1605, led to the discovery of the Gunpowder Plot and the grim deaths of the plotters. There is some evidence to suggest that it came from Dorothy Selby and legend has it that she was walled up in the cupboard as a punishment by friends of the plotters.

Could this have been the woman of Pat's dream and was this just a nightmare brought on by half-hearing the legends of the old house? But there was more to Pat's ordeal than a nightmare.

'I threw the piece of fireplace away,' she said, 'but it was no use. The next morning six crystal glasses were smashed and the stems stood in a row on the table. Each day something was destroyed. On the sixth day two precious ivory statuettes were destroyed. My husband was frightened though I didn't tell him about the woman I had seen.

'On the seventh day I thought it was all right till I found my amethyst necklace I always wore round my neck was missing and had been ripped in half. Soon after I ended my marriage and moved out of the house and so far the woman hasn't followed me. But her cries still haunt me.'

I discussed this case with a psychologist who does not want to be named for professional reasons as she was commenting on people she had never met. In her opinion, the cause of the destruction might have been more earthly than supernatural; she thought the husband was probably breaking the things for spite and the wife, who felt guilty for stealing the stone, had projected her own helplessness about her situation on to a figure from the past to avoid acknowledging it. But, as with all rational explanations, the 'common-sense' answers never quite fit.

Why, for instance, did Pat's husband get worried about the breakages if he was the one responsible for it? Could it be just coincidence that the breakages started as soon as Pat had stolen the stone? Or did some ancient ghost latch on to her and the souvenir she took, following her back into suburbia which was no longer quite so safe for Pat? My own feeling is that the truth could lie somewhere between the two theories.

Sometimes the supernatural takes the blame for something we or someone else has done. It's easier that way —

like sitting back and waiting for our fortune to be made because we have been promised by a gypsy fortune teller that we will inherit money. But sometimes the supernatural can take a hand even though we do not want to acknowledge it because it will upset our safe, comfortable, logical lives.

For Pat, the process, although painful and terrifying, was at least cleansing for it brought matters to a head and she has moved away from a relationship which was intolerable.

But you do not have to import the supernatural into suburbia from an old dark house. Many ghosts seem to be attached to a particular place and, like it or not, when we move into Dunroamin or Bella Vista we can inherit other people's family spirits along with the dubious plumbing and bad wiring. The occult can intrude into the most modern housing estate and even follow you across the sea. In 1994 a Vietnamese couple with eight children were rehoused by Newham Council, in east London, after they said that their four-bedroom council house in Canning Town was possessed by ancestral spirits. The mother had blamed a suicide attempt by her 16-year-old daughter, and the collapse of a younger girl, on their dead relatives.

There was some dismay among councillors who felt that moving a family on these grounds might lead to accusations of queue-jumping. And, as one councillor said, 'How do we know that the spirits are not going to follow this family to their new home?'

A spokeswoman for the council would not discuss the reasons for the move in detail but said that the family was being moved because of overcrowding, 'although manifestation of spirits is part of the Vietnamese culture and must be respected'.

Unless you have a sympathetic council or estate agent, then you may well have to listen to the moans of your invisible neighbours and former residents, or simply watch them as they go about the daily business of yesterday. Even if you've bought a brand new des. res. you're not immune because it may have been built on the site of an earlier house where the ghost once lived. I knew of a lady in Wokingham, Berkshire, who found, when she moved to a new executive estate, that she had a resident phantom monk. The land had once belonged to a mediaeval priory.

Diane in Gwent told me that she has been putting up with just such a problem for 16 years, ever since she moved into a house on a big estate in Gwent on land which had once belonged to a manor house. Now, she says, she has got used to the spirit. 'I say to it "For goodness sake be quiet or you will have to go".

'The first night we shut the lounge door and there was a tremendous banging, as if someone was trying to come in. We were frightened but when we opened the door there was nothing there and there was no wind. But the door kept shuddering.

'We now keep it open all the time.

'One night my husband and I were lying in bed when we heard galloping horses on the landing.

'One day my son came into the kitchen absolutely terrified saying something white had followed him downstairs. I went upstairs and passed through the entity on the landing. Three weeks later, my daughter who was fifteen and a half came to our bedroom at around midnight, absolutely hysterical. She said that she had woken up and a man had been there in her bedroom just staring at her. She'd hidden under the blankets and when she opened her eyes he was gone.

'If I close my bedroom door I hear knocking as though someone is trying to get in. The thing seems centred round my bedroom so I redecorated it and put a peacock chair in the corner. But it was creaking and moving all night and we had to take it downstairs.

'I collect face masks made of ceramic. One evening the two above the settee that were hooked over on a ribbon flew off into the middle of the floor . But the hook stayed on the wall.

'A month ago, my husband had gone into my son's room during the night because the boy was upset. I felt someone holding me on the bed. I could feel a leg over my leg and an arm pressing my arm. It happened a second time when I was on my own. And the following morning I had fingermarks and scratches under the skin on my inner thigh.

'This really frightened me and my mother-in-law, who is religious, has suggested I call a minister. I spoke to a white voodooist by telephone after seeing him on a television programme and he said there were evil spirits who were making things go wrong in our life.

'Certainly things have gone very wrong. We have all been constantly ill and my husband has lost two jobs.

'People say "Why don't you move?" but we can't afford to.'

A ghost does not have to have any particular connection to your house. The phantom might just take a liking to your home as Ron, who lives in Godalming in Surrey, told me.

'Two years ago I used to hear noises on the stairs at night similar to footsteps when the children had gone to bed and the house was quiet. My wife also heard them but we didn't mention them to each other until later.

'There was a bedroom we never used and so the door

was always kept closed. But every morning it was always open.

'One day my wife was alone in the house. She had washed her hair and was sitting at the dressing table when something touched her hair. It felt very human but there was nothing there.

'She phoned me at work — but I know she's mad,' he said, jokingly, 'so I didn't take much notice. Two weeks later she was standing at the sink in the kitchen. And she felt it touch her hair again. This time she was annoyed and told it in no uncertain terms to go away.

'We had a long lounge and we did not draw the curtains on a big window leading to the garden. I used to see a grey misty shape looking over my left shoulder reflected in the mirror. It would stay there even if we talked about it. But if someone moved it would go *whoosh!* out of the door.

'It was just like having someone friendly living in the house but I wanted to understand why it was there.

'We rang up the local vicar, who wasn't a great deal of help, so I mentioned it to some friends who said they knew some spiritualists who might be able to help. I was very sceptical but three very nice ladies came with pendulums. They walked around the house and told me which parts the spirits liked.

'They went into my son's bedroom and gave my wife the pendulum and she found it moving in very strange ways. I used to see the spirit next to my nine-year-old son Ben's bed when he was asleep. The children had been aware of something but they hadn't said anything.

'The spiritualists said we could communicate with the spirit. I was very sceptical but we all sat there and it spoke through the chief medium. The spirit said she was a European woman who had died in the 1920s. She'd been

30

about to get married but, coming home from a party, she'd fallen into a lily pond and drowned.

'So I asked her why she had come to us and she said she'd been looking for somewhere large and bright and white to live. We lived in a large white detached house so she had moved in where she had always wanted to go. We felt we shouldn't keep her so the spiritualists cleared the room, opened the front door and she went. But we felt she was part of our life.

'It's opened a new perspective to use because it's not the sort of thing people talk about although since then I have found that many of my friends have had experiences.

'The spiritualists said that they found the hardest ghosts to get rid of were those that had died when they were drunk. They had had to deal with a ghost who used to sit on a stone outside a house. Apparently he had been sitting there for 300 years because he had died drunk and had not realised that he had died. The spiritualists had had a terrific job convincing him that he was dead.'

If you like a pint before your Sunday lunch, you may find it a bit disconcerting to find a load of Quakers sitting round the table when you return home for the Sunday roast. It was not the first psychic experience for David Bryan, whom we met at the start of this book. He wrote to the Alister Hardy Research Centre:

'It was on Sunday February 12, 1989. My wife Linda and myself came home Sunday dinner time from the Leebridge Tavern. We walked into our kitchen to find these people sitting at our kitchen table. They were dressed in Quaker clothes, a man, a woman and a young girl about 12 or 13 years of age. Linda started shouting and swearing at them asking how they got into our house as it was locked and bolted. I told her to shut up as I realised they were spirit

31

people but they were solid as you and me.

'They talked to us for some time — for about 20 minutes — then they vanished. To this very day neither Linda nor I can remember what we talked about. I wonder if it would be possible to be hypnotised to find what it was all about?'

David's letter was passed on to me and I was able as a Brummie and a Quaker to offer a few suggestions. Birmingham was a great centre of Quakerism and I'd come across Quaker ghosts before at other Quaker centres (one woman told me how, when she was a little girl she saw them in her bedroom. Her mother saw them too but denied this for years afterwards because she didn't want to frighten her daughter[1]).

I was able to reassure David that Quakers, phantom or otherwise, were peace-loving people and it was probably some anniversary for that particular group. Perhaps they'd had a house on the same spot. We don't ever know for sure why ghosts return, but Quaker ghosts do tend to come back to peaceful households. These days they're not so worried about the temperance aspect, so I didn't recommend that David signed the pledge immediately to avoid lectures from spirits on the evils of spirits. After all, he had already had one warning from his White Lady of Hockley. The Quakers must have been well pleased with his conduct because they did not lecture him at the time and have not returned.

From industrial Birmingham to Portsmouth where I spoke to Andrea during a radio-phone-in programme about her ghostly sitting tenants. 'I am 37 now,' she said, 'but the trouble with ghostly neighbours began when I was

---

[1] This story appears in *The Psychic Power of Children* published by Foulsham

only eight years old. I saw a ghost in our house which absolutely terrified me. It was not till years later I found out my brother had seen the figure too. He described in detail what he had seen and I realised it was the same man. It was strange we never told each other.

'The ghost seemed an ordinary enough man like lots of others round our way except for the fact that he wore gangster type clothing, a dark brown double breasted coat, long and belted at the waist and a big Al Capone-type hat pulled over his eyes.

'Several years later we moved to another part of Portsmouth and met a couple who used to live near our old house but had moved away years before. As we got chatting, it turned out the woman's family had lived in the house next to my old one for years before we'd lived there. She said our house had a bit of a reputation in the old days. The man who had lived in our old house in the nineteen thirties had committed suicide. Her mother had always said he was a bit of a wide boy and used to dress up in gangster-type clothes which had shocked the neighbours because it was a very respectable area.'

Andrea's next ghostly tenant appeared when she was grown up and living in another house. 'We bought our house off the son of an old man who had recently died in his eighties. The son lived further down the road and we got on well. One night I dreamed of a man doing a Scottish reel with a very tiny man in sailor's uniform. The little man danced the sailor's hornpipe. They were both so happy. The dream was so real but I had no idea who they could be. Quite by chance the next day I was chatting to the man from whom we had bought the house and I mentioned the dream.

'He went white and told me: "The small man was my

Uncle Dink. We called him that because he was so small. He used to be a sailor and my dad used to dance the Scottish reels with him when I was a kid and he used to come to the house." '

Don, who lives on the Isle of Wight, feared he was going insane as a teenager when his family moved house and he started seeing things. 'In my new bedroom I used to see a woman outside my window night after night staring in and waving to me. She had grey hair and a mint-coloured dress.

'One night I was determined to find out whether I was dreaming and so I lit a cigarette when I saw her and put it into the ash tray. I never smoked in bed but I felt that would be a test. The cigarette was still there the next morning. But if I wasn't dreaming then what? I didn't feel I could tell my parents but I needed to talk to someone about the old woman. We'd become very friendly with the man who lived next door and so I decided to confide in him.

' "You're going to think I'm barmy," I said, "but I keep seeing this old woman staring into my bedroom window and waving." I described her and he smiled. "You're seeing old Vera," he told me.

'He explained that Vera had lived in his house and when her husband became ill, Vera often came to the window to wave to Jimmy, the old man who had my bedroom, to get him to go over and help. The old woman had died not long after her husband. We'd bought the house off Jimmy's people after he died. Old Vera was a familiar sight.'

So perhaps we shouldn't talk about haunted, but inhabited, houses and accept that other people's families, like our own, may be forever.

It can be something in our own family that triggers off

the dead person's actions. Shirley is a medium from Leeds. In my book, *The Psychic Power of Children,* she described how her own mother had punished her for talking about ghosts she could see in her house and so she was determined her own children's visions would be accepted. And it seemed to be the children that roused the maternal instinct in the resident ghost.

Shirley explained: 'I used to hear and see an old lady going from the back to the front of the house upstairs during the night. My son slept in the back bedroom and my daughter in the front.

'So I decided to make a few inquiries from elderly neighbours and one of them told me that the lady who had the house before me and was now died used to regularly go from the back bedroom where she'd slept and check her daughter in the front bedroom. The child had been ill quite a lot, so the mum was up and down all night for years. As the children grew older, the old lady's visits stopped.'

Coral's ghost too was attracted by her infant: 'My son was two months old. One night he was ill and I was lying awake feeling very worried. During the night an elderly man appeared. I tried to nudge my husband awake but couldn't move. The old man stood looking into the cot. I wasn't frightened, in fact his presence was very reassuring, and I stopped feeling anxious about my son as I felt he was cared for.

'I wondered whether it might be the old man who used to live in our house before his death. When I asked around I discovered he had always loved children. Some time later his son called at our house and I was struck by the resemblance between him and the ghost of the old man. But I never told him or his family about the visitation.'

So you may not need bell, book and candle if you make

a few inquiries of the old duck down the road. And when you discover why your ghost walks you may be happy to keep it. It could even add thousands to the value of your house. On the other hand, once the purpose of the visit is understood it often disappears.

Vivien Greene, widow of the late author Graham Greene, told me of a ghost she had seen years before. Though her home is set back from the road and contains a beautiful Victorian dolls house museum in the grounds, the area is strangely suburban. Here, the old Oxford countryside, with its locks and leafy walks, merges into the modern world of a new estate only a mile away. But it was in the gracious surroundings of yesteryear, as we sat among her treasures, that she shared her experience:

'Before I was married I was living with my friends, the Weavers at 10 Holyrood Street in Oxford. My room faced New College Gate. It was an old house with a well in the middle that was used as a trolley for taking laundry up and down. At the side was a deep cupboard about 10 feet long that Stella kept clothes in. But she always put a chair against it because it frightened her.

'Because she was having a baby she wanted to move out of the room so I moved into it. The room was on the third floor and I still put a chair in front of the cupboard.

'One night I was totally asleep when I was suddenly aware that sitting by my bed was a nurse. She was Scottish-looking with gingery hair and one gold tooth at the side of her mouth. She was smiling at me which was how I saw the tooth. The room was very black but she was like a colour photo against the blackness. I hid under the blankets until I was so stifled I had to put my head out again. She was still there. I don't know whether I was so exhausted I just fell asleep or whether I fainted. But she had quite a pleasant smile.

'Afterwards I was not frightened to sleep in the room in spite of my experience.'

So domestic ghosts needn't be scary if we think of them just as carrying on their own routine alongside ours. After all we are the ghosts of tomorrow and if we fancy coming back to tend the roses we don't want someone trying to exorcise us.

It seems that the suburbs, villages and cities are bursting with ghosts and yet in certain places a ghostly presence is so strong that it may be seen by several people independently. Bridget worked as a chamber maid in a hotel in Bournemouth. She used to cross Boscombe Gardens early in the morning to get to work. She told me: 'One morning my path was blocked by a nun in an old-fashioned black habit.

'I said, "Excuse me" but she kept darting from side to side and her face was quite demented. I was petrified because I couldn't shake her off but then I realised she wasn't trying to hurt me but to get away herself.

'When I got to work I was shaking and blurted out my story to one of the old staff at the hotel. She told me that she had seen the nun herself and that many years before one of the hotels on the Square had been a TB home for nuns. But after that I always walked round the edge of the square though I never saw her again.'

When Alf and Mabel moved into a big house in Twickenham as handyman and housekeeper to two elderly sisters, they discovered the ghostly residents more troublesome than their new employers. They'd applied for the job because they were tired of living in their cramped house in Woodley, Berkshire, with noisy neighbours, and fancied somewhere a bit more select.

Alf explained about the first night at Twickenham: 'It was a cold and damp March night and Mabel and I were shivering in the old groom's quarters, wishing we'd stayed in Woodley. Mabel had dropped off to sleep but I was too cold. Suddenly an old woman with iron grey hair walked through the wall and into my room. The light shone through her and she had an evil looking face, "Get out, get out of this house!" she screamed.

'She wore a black dress with starched collar and pearl buttons on the cuff. I was terrified and called out to Mabel. Then, with a final malevolent look, she disappeared through the wall again. Mabel is normally a light sleeper but I had the devil's job to wake her. She just said I'd had a nightmare and must have been drinking. But I hadn't even touched so much as a glass of sherry and I hadn't gone to sleep.

'The next day I was talking to a middle-aged chap in the corner shop. I mentioned where I was working and he said, "You won't get much sleep there."

'I asked him what he meant and he said his brother had worked there and several times had seen a woman come through the wall and told him to get out. The figure had iron grey hair and wore a black dress. The brother had got another job as soon as possible.

'I inquired from an old woman who lived nearby — I didn't like to ask my employers — and the women did have a very elderly relative who'd lived there when they were young, who became confused and would try to throw family members on to the street at night. It had been quite a local talking point. Mabel was still cynical.

'But then she started to hear heavy footsteps on the floor above though it was locked and no longer used. So eventually I found a pretext to get the key off the owners and next time we heard the footsteps we went up. There was no one and all over the floor was a fine white dust and not a single footprint. As soon as possible I got a new job and went back to noisy living neighbours.'

The ghost which upset Alf and Mabel was unpleasant but harmless. More sinister was the being which disturbed the pleasant and relatively uncomplicated life of Maria, a young accountant from the north of England. She had never experienced anything out of the ordinary until she stayed at a hotel in the country with her boyfriend. During the night she felt some malevolent force trying to take her over. Maria said she felt an intense physical pain as the power went from her head to her feet. She felt she was fighting for her life.

Her boyfriend woke and saw a strange light round her but thought he was dreaming.

The experience left Maria feeling totally drained and ill. So she contacted the local Catholic priest who told her it was her own fault for sinning with her boyfriend.

Maria was too ill to return to work. She contacted the Alister Hardy Research Centre and was put in touch with me. When I spoke to her she said that she felt the presence was in some way involved with the hotel at which she had stayed, but she was afraid that the thing might have followed her in some way. Until that time she had totally disbelieved in the paranormal and her experience had shattered the certainty of her world.

Why, she wanted to know had it happened? I didn't feel it would be particularly helpful to research the history of the hotel. The management had denied that the hotel had any connection with the paranormal. This would not be surprising even if they had known about it. Unlike a friendly phantom cavalier, the more unpleasant psychic

39

manifestations are not good for business. And such notes of such things were hardly likely to be left in the visitors' book.

There was also a strong possibility that any incident which had left this legacy of evil in the room might not have been recorded anyway. Perhaps two lovers had quarrelled violently in that room. Or it might have been inhabited by a jealous old spinster who'd been rejected in love and whose bitterness had imprinted itself on the walls.

But even if you could find a story which fitted the bill you could never know for certain that it was the right one.

What I felt was the most important factor in this case was that Maria had stayed in the same room the following night and yet nothing further had happened. Nor had she had any trouble since, although the fear that something might re-emerge was obviously playing on her mind.

I felt that in this case she could probably give herself a clean psychic bill of health. As a bonus, I suggested that she now had a wider understanding of the world and that contrary to her fears, she wouldn't start seeing ghosts on every corner if she didn't want to, which she said she didn't.

She had already discovered she wasn't alone in her experience. On impulse, Maria had confided in a partner with her firm who, contrary to her fear, did not dismiss her story as rubbish but said he'd had psychic experiences himself.

It is hard to talk about psychic events, especially if they have strong negative aspects. But there are an awful lot of people who have had them and it can be helpful to shed the taboos. After all, if half the population is walking around with a hidden psychic experience then a lot of energy is wasted preserving the secrets of the majority.

But it's not easy talking about psychic experiences. Even clairvoyants often ask me not to use family names when repeating personal experiences to avoid embarrassment. I've had heads of psychic organisations saying the same. It's on trains and in parks when you just get chatting the real psychic world peeps out, especially if you agree to keep names and addresses secret and do so.

During one such encounter, Pam, a former nurse, told me about her haunted house and the trouble began almost as soon as the family moved in. 'I was living in an old house in Farnborough. The roof had burned down and had been rebuilt just before we moved in. There was lots of dark brown paint everywhere. But it wasn't just that. The house felt wrong though I couldn't explain to my sceptical husband.

'One day soon after we'd arrived I was peeling the potatoes and putting them into a bowl of water. I was using a very sharp knife. When I'd finished, I put the knife high up on a cupboard. I'd got small children so always double-checked. Then I wrapped the peelings in newspaper and opened the pedal bin with my toe.

'As I bent down to put the peelings in, I saw a glint of metal in the bin. It was the knife pointing up towards me, carefully hidden in the rubbish so only the point showed. Had I put the newspaper with the peelings in the bin, the knife would have gone straight into my hand. When I looked on top of the cupboard, the knife had gone.

'A week later my sister came for the housewarming. "Put your coat upstairs," I told her as I was carrying a plate of sausage rolls through into the dining room.

'A couple of minutes later my no-nonsense sister was back with her coat. "I can't go past the corner of the stairs," she told me. "Please walk up with me."

'There was an overhead skylight at the top of the stairs and we could see a big dark shadowy thing looming there though it was brilliant sunshine. There were no trees close, nothing that could cause the shadow. The shadow stayed for weeks.

'Even my husband didn't like it. I went to see a Jesuit priest because I was so scared. He sprinkled holy water in the hall but added, "It's probably your age and imagination."

'But the thing remained malevolent and hovering. Sunshine or shower, it was there and there were no buildings, no posts, no fences, nothing to explain it though my husband tried. I could feel its malevolence and feared for the children. So one evening without telling Pete I went to a healer who belonged to a healing circle in Berkhamstead.

'Pete stayed home with the kids. I knew he would get upset and tell me not to dabble even though he had had a bad experience the night before. Pete had woken about three in the morning with a terrified feeling. Though he wasn't religious, he told me he has gone round making the sign of the cross over me and the children and had watched us till morning.

'He decided to lay a new stair carpet to try to brighten the place — he still couldn't cope with the idea the problem might not be of this world.

'That night I sat in the healing circle and we all held hands. As Bob started to exorcise the spirit, his voice changed as if it came from the depths of the earth. Suddenly I was standing in the middle of my hall and a gale was blowing. It died down and it was just like a spring day in the house. The time was about 9.30. I checked my

42

watch afterwards.

'When I got home, Pete was waiting as white as a sheet and very shaken. He told me between stutters. "About half past nine I was laying the stair carpet when suddenly all the doors in the house started to bang and rattle. I thought one of the kids had left the doors open. But when I checked they were all bolted. Then suddenly I found myself standing in a spring day."

'After that there was no more trouble and the shadow disappeared even on the darkest day. But Pete to this day will try to explain it away logically.'

Perhaps we should check the vibes of a property before we put down a deposit as well as the decor and dry rot. Sometimes a house will cause problems for tenant after tenant, while others get along fine, just as some neighbours will blend perfectly and others constantly rub each other up the wrong way. One family will run screaming from a haunted house, while another stays for decades without hearing so much as a paranormal creak.

So if a house feels wrong for you, don't buy it — no matter if the estate agent is waving the best deal ever in your direction. Animals instinctively won't settle where it feels alien. Obviously you can't take the cat house-hunting, but trust your own instinctive radar to guide you.

If in doubt about the psychic credentials of a property, you could get it blessed by your church. In an extreme case you might like to have the road exorcised, for it is not only the old country tracks once travelled by highwaymen that give trouble. The North Circular Road, always packed with traffic as it winds its way round London may seem an unlikely place for an exorcism. But that is what happened in October, 1992.

James Kwesi Simpson who was 28 and a postal worker

from Golders Green died as he climbed over a barrier outside his house and was hit by a juggernaut. His family who come from the Ivory Coast, got permission from the Department of Transport to perform a ritual exorcism on the spot he died. A Ghanaian spiritual healer performed the ceremony.

Traffic police directed traffic round the mourners at midnight since traffic was still quite heavy. Gertrude, the dead man's sister said that such ceremonies were customary in her culture. "We needed to free his spirit otherwise other drivers might have seen it on the road as they were going along and it could have caused accidents," she told reporters.

These ceremonies are not unique to Ghana. The Reverend Tom Willis, is Vicar of Sowerby, near Bridlington, and an official exorcist to the Diocese of York. Mr Willis, a sensible, sympathetic father of five, believes that areas of road can bear the scars of past tragedy.

'Sometimes where there's been an accident there is a mental telerecording by either someone involved or a witness and that stays in the spot and is seen by people periodically.

'For example a taxi driver went up a road in Hull and just opposite the bridge over the River Hull a man ran out in front of the taxi. The driver hit him and got out but could see no one. Fearing that the man was under the taxi he reversed but still the road was empty.

'Without fetching the fare he went straight back to the depot in a state of shock. A second driver went out and the same thing happened.

'Maybe the horror left by the driver involved in the original crash is now a barrier. People can pick up distant memories that seem to keep certain anniversaries or certain times of day. If you pray at the spot and ask for the peace of God to return to the place then it is not seen again. I believe that if you can cure the problem, then the diagnosis must be near the truth.'

But exorcisms are not always necessary. We can happily share our location with this other world so long as we remember that paranormal neighbours and sitting tenants are no more considerate than earthly ones. The former inhabitants of your house may drop in at entirely the wrong time, perhaps when you are in the bath — or worse still on the loo.

Geoff and Carol moved into the top floor flat of an old house in Bath Road, Reading, when they were first married. The toilet was a bit of a trek down a long corridor. One morning at about 5am Geoff went to the loo. Men can be notorious for taking their time in the littlest room but when he hadn't returned after half an hour, his wife felt she should investigate.

Carol found Geoff sitting there frozen with shock. He told her a woman wearing a long grey dress had appeared, thrown back her head and laughed at him and then disappeared into thin air.

Chapter Three

Voices Of The Dead

He, being white, cannot hear the voice of those that died.Tell me Tuan,' he went on, looking at Lingard with curiosity — 'tell me, Tuan, do you white people ever hear the voices of the invisible ones?'

'We do not,' answered Lingard, 'because those that we cannot see do not speak.'

'Never speak! And never complain with sounds that are not words,' exclaimed Babalatchi, doubtingly. 'It may be so — or your ears are dull. We Malays hear many sounds near the places where men are buried . . . but I do not want to hear the complaint of invisible lips. Therefore I go.'

*From **An Outcast of the Islands** by Joseph Conrad*

CONRAD'S BOOK IS set in the last century in the Malayan jungle, a primitive place where a belief in ghosts could flourish. But the brusque declaration of Lingard, the totally practical sea captain, missed the whole point of ghostly encounters. For as we have seen, some people, even in suburbia, see ghosts wherever they go while other people could have one sitting on the settee next to them and not notice.

One theory I have is that if you aren't worried by the idea of ghosts, then you don't block out what may be a natural instinctive ability to see them. Hence children don't have any problems with the psychic and some people grow up in sympathetic households and don't ever allow the left brain bit to contradict the evidence of their senses. And so a 'psychic family' may simply be an ordinary family whose boundaries of reality are slightly wider than average.

But even those of us who have a barrier to seeing ghosts, even on the ghost train at the local fair, can suddenly become receptive in times of great personal stress. Hence people going through a separation, divorce or job crisis suddenly discover untapped psychic powers. And once you've seen one ghost, you get a habit for it. In the case of Julia Harris who lives in Reading, she was feeling pretty worried because she was going for her first job when her psychic ability went walkabout. She told me about this first sighting as we sat in her kitchen drinking coffee, while my younger two took advantage of her children's play equipment.

'When I was sixteen in the early 1970s I went to work at Satchwell's in Slough. The firm used to make things during the war for the Army. As I went in, I noticed ahead of me a woman dressed in a nineteen-forties style dress and shoes. As this was back in fashion at the time, I just thought she looked rather nice. I followed her up the stairs to the office. She went straight in but I popped into the loo to check I looked all right. When I went into the office, she had gone. I mentioned to the girl at the desk how much I liked the cerise dress the woman was wearing who came in before me.

' "No one's been in here this morning," the girl told me. An older woman behind the counter asked me to describe the woman and I mentioned the forties style dress and wedge heels and bobbed hair.

'She told me, "A woman was killed here during a raid in the war. People say they see her around in a cerise dress. But I thought it was just a story."'

'It wasn't a good start to my new job.'

But the majority of ghosts who appear in Psychic Suburbia are not strangers, nor the headless horsemen of fairy tales. Most are family members.

Jane, who lives in Bournemouth, told me the following story. 'When I was young my grandad lived with us. He became very ill and one night died quite suddenly. Dad didn't want to upset his sister by waking her in the night with bad news. So next morning he went round to her house. But his dad had beaten him to it.

' "Dad's dead," she said as she opened the door. "I couldn't sleep last night and Dad appeared at my bedside. He told me, 'I'm all right now, love,' and he was gone." Her father had appeared to her at the exact time that he had died.'

Margaret Birchenough was nurse at a hospital in a small town in Yorkshire. She and her husband had been away for three weeks but came back in time for the Great Yorkshire Show, a favourite event in Margaret's calendar. The Show was held at Harrogate, some distance from her home.

Margaret recalled: 'My husband had gone off to buy something and I was waiting at the back of some tents. I was suddenly aware of someone coming up behind me and, thinking my husband had been remarkably quick, I turned round. But it was a former colleague, Mr McKewan, a surgeon whom I had worked with before his retirement, who was coming towards me, smiling in his usual friendly way.

' "How are you, Margaret?" he asked. "So good to see

48

you again."

' "I'm very well," I replied. "I'm just waiting for my husband,"

'And at that moment my husband arrived and I said, "You must let me introduce Mr McKewan," because the two men had never met. We stood chatting for a while and then the surgeon shook hands with my husband.

' "It was a real pleasure working with your Margaret," he said. "You must be very proud of her." '

The surgeon touched Margaret's hand then disappeared into the crowd.

Soon afterwards, Margaret met a nurse friend and mentioned she had seen Mr McKewan at the show. The friend said she must have been mistaken because Mr McKewan had died two weeks before while Margaret was away. But Margaret says it was no mistake.

'And his hand was quite warm. I shall never forget what was a chance to say goodbye in such a happy way. He was as real as you or I.'

I first met Margaret in Oxford. When she came on holiday to the Isle of Wight, she asked to meet again at Alum Bay the local pleasure park. In her forthright way she insisted I spoke to the coach driver on the telephone to arrange a meeting place. She said that if I used her story I was to mention that her late husband was a master cheese maker, as she was very proud of him and wanted him remembered in some way. Margaret's sister, whom I met along with half the coach party, wrote recently to tell me that Margaret had died, so I hope that she and her husband are together again.

Nurses do make very strong bonds sometimes with patients and a patient may want to say goodbye. I met Connie in Bournemouth and she told me how when she was nursing in a care home she became very attached an elderly Jewish gentleman.

'One night I had a vivid dream of a skull cap flying through the air,' she said. 'It was so real that I woke and looked at the clock. The next morning, when I went into work, I discovered that my old Jewish friend, who hadn't even been ill, had died in the night at the time I woke from the dream. I believe he came to say goodbye.'

As well as bringing news of death, ghosts can sometimes bring comfort, particularly to a member of the family who might feel guilty for some reason about the death. I heard this story from Trina a neighbour from the time when I lived in Woodley, near Reading in Berkshire. We shared the school run, depending on whose car would start that morning — we both had high mortgages and skimped a bit on regular services. She told me the story one day while we were having coffee and bemoaning the expense of kids.

'The night my elderly mother died of hypothermia she had turned the heating in her sheltered flat right down. There had been no need because the bills were paid for her but Mum had started to get confused. I'd checked on her during the evening as usual and everything had been fine. I was the last person to see Mum alive. I missed her desperately and kept reliving the last meeting over and over again. If only I'd checked her again that night.

'A few weeks later I was lying on the settee alone at home during the day, having a rest as I hadn't been sleeping well since Mum had gone. When I was a little girl I had very long hair and my mum used to plait it and she would stroke my hair very gently. As I lay there I suddenly felt someone stroking my hair very gently and I knew it was my mum telling me it was all right and there wasn't

50

anything I could have done differently. But then you think maybe it's just imagination.

'Later in the month I went to a psychic healer for the first time as I had back trouble. As I walked across the room, I felt what I thought was a cobweb touching my hair but when I looked up there was nothing. "That's your mum come to say hello," the healer said and it all made sense. I hadn't told her anything about Mum — in fact she didn't know me from Adam as she lived in Tilehurst the other side of Reading.'

Sometimes, even if we accept the death of a loved one, it is good to feel their assurance and approval not in world-shattering ways but in the down to earth practical signs of caring.

Pat, who comes from Bromley, told me: 'I was at my mum's house a few months after she died, on my hands and knees polishing the floor. I'd tried to take care of dad and keep the place up to scratch after Mum went. It seemed the least I could do. But it wasn't easy as I wasn't domesticated like Mum. I looked up and there was Mum at the top of the stairs smiling down at me. She always used to say she liked to see her face in the hall floor. I think she was pleased I was doing it so well and looking after my dad.'

We talk of 'seeing' ghosts but the contact need not be visual or even tied to a particular sensory path. The sixth sense is not dependent on more conventional channels. Jean Griffin, who has been blind for many years, told me how her partially sighted friend came back to see her after his death. Arthur appeared to her shortly after his death when she was living in Cowes on the Isle of Wight. The town is famed for its glamorous yacht races but, when you get away from the sea front, it is in fact a remarkably ordinary — but very pleasant — town of semis and terraces. While I was talking to Jean, it became clear that her intuition is very highly developed and she says that she can sum people and situations up in moments and is invariably proved right.

'I had shared a house with Arthur for many years though we had our own separate flats,' she told me. 'Arthur died suddenly from a heart attack. His little cat, Suzy, grieved very much and insisted on staying in his flat and I would go in and feed her and fuss her. One day when I went in, I felt a force blocking my way. It was as though someone was standing in front of me though when I put out my hand there was no solid form.

' "It's Arthur," I told Suzy, and I felt his presence there with me very strongly. It was an immensely reassuring experience. But when I went back into his flat later he had gone and it never happened there again. I have since married and am living several miles away from the old house but I still think of Arthur and sometimes know he is with me and I say his name.'

Even those who have eyes and a flexible attitude towards the supernatural may not necessarily see ghosts. Instead they may hear phantom voices.

The comedian, Benny Hill, who had a very close relationship with his parents, once said that whenever he went to lay flowers on their grave at the cemetery in Shirley, near Southampton, he felt he could hear them talking.

His mother would always say: 'You've spent £12 on a bunch of flowers. You shouldn't waste your money.'

'My father was always a great man for doing everything himself. And when I'm messing up the flowers — breaking their stems — I can hear him saying: "Oh give me that. Here let me do it.''

'When my father died I wept buckets but when my mother died I hardly cried at all. Perhaps it was guilt because although I loved both my parents very much I was always closer to my mother and perhaps my tears at my father's death were partly guilt because I didn't love him as much as my mother.'

Sceptics will say that the voices were conjured up inside his head from memories of his parents. It is true that if we know people well we can predict their reactions to a situation, and can sometimes repeat word for word in advance what they will say when we give them a piece of news.

Mr Hill's untimely death prevented me from ever asking him whether he sided with the sceptics or the believers on this issue. And as he never knew me personally I do not think that he would bother to return from wherever he is now just to give me his opinion.

But the sceptical point of view does not get full support of the Reverend Tom Willis. 'Sometimes granny will come back for a reason,' he told me, 'for example, to tell the family where the will is. The good dead also offer protection in times of danger. Psychiatrists and psychologists will dismiss this as your subconscious telling you what do and the mind projecting the information into granny's voice. But such explanations just don't ring true. Grannies especially can get very protective.'

He does not see such encounters with the supernatural as necessarily a cause for bell, book and candle but calls them contact with 'the good dead'. Mr Willis is quick to reassure terrified parishioners that in some cases a ghostly presence may just be Aunty or Gran popping back for a visit. He told me of one such case: 'A woman asked for my help because she was terrified when she saw a woman's figure at the foot of her bed. I reassured her it was either connected with the house or a family appearance. She'd lived in the house for twenty five years and never seen anything before.

'So I asked her to describe what she had seen. There was an aura of red, she told me, and the figure was wearing a kilt. I asked if anyone had died recently in the family who wore a kilt. At first she said no, then she remembered. "My cousin died recently. She used to wear a kilt and a lot of red. But why should she come to me?"

' "Have you been in touch with your aunt recently?" I asked. She hadn't so I suggested maybe she should give her aunt a ring and see if everything was all right.

'The Church talks of the Communion of Saints, which is the fellowship of all the people of God worshipping together, both those who are living and those who are dead. They are brought together in worship. I often think of the John Betjeman poem of the old lady at the altar rail with her dead family drawn close around her. I know I feel closer to my deceased relatives at the altar rail.

'The good dead do try not to disturb us when they visit. I know some clergy think it's rather dubious and can encourage other things. But I believe that if good results then it must be a good thing. I know if I died, I'd want to come and see my kids.'

Grandmothers do not just return to see how we are getting on but sometimes to offer advice — if we are wise enough to take it. Before the last war, Ron was living in the Home Counties His gran's ghost came back as a warning to his mother but she didn't understand the message that might, perhaps, have saved years of heartache.

He recalled: 'Her two sisters were asleep but mother

heard footsteps on the stairs and saw a flickering light as a figure entered the room. It was her deceased mother. My mother was petrified. The figure pointed at one of the two sisters before vanishing. But my mother did not understand what her mother meant.

'Mother could not pay the rent so we had to go and live with one of the sisters. We were very unhappy with the sister my mother chose and when I was nine we went to live with the other sister, the one my dead grandma had pointed to. Though we were very poor we were very happy indeed with her.'

Communication from beyond can be difficult. For every full-blown message come tappings, scents, elusive hints that have to be pieced together like a jigsaw puzzle. The deceased, especially in their passing, do seem to enjoy a certain amount of stage effects, stopping clocks, crashing phone stands, perhaps the modern day equivalent of passing knells.

Until I began to research this book, I had not realised what a noisy business passing over could be. One of the first cases I came across was of a girl who heard lots of tiny hammers banging in the kitchen though the house was deserted except for her mother and herself. There were no neighbouring walls. Minutes later, news came her gran had unexpectedly died. The mother wasn't surprised and hadn't even left the comfort of her chair to check. Apparently the noise of hammers was a family tradition at the time of a family member going over.

I enjoy psychic teasers but I can't make head nor tail of the story of old Ben Brown. So I include it here and hope someone reading the book will get the answer in one. Ben Brown was the village cobbler when Lesley was young. Lesley who now lives in Southampton recalls: 'My father was very ill in hospital and one day when my mother and I visited him, he said, "Look there's old Ben Brown," and he nodded his head in greeting to a bed on the opposite side of the ward.

'But there was no Ben Brown. Dad insisted he'd had a good chat to Ben and we went along with what Dad said as we knew he was dying and indeed he did die soon after seeing Ben. Sixteen years later my brother had a serious operation and was in the same ward as the one in which my father had died, in fact in almost the identical spot. I visited him one afternoon and suddenly it sounded just as if my father was speaking. "Look there's old Ben Brown."

'I was shaken because when I looked opposite there was the old man himself, aged about 86 by now. I went over and had a chat to him but he was all ready for an operation and a bit sleepy but he remembered me. My brother survived but I can't explain it though somewhere there must be an explanation.'

A living ghost, an astral projection? I found the story among some very old records and the people had moved on. Perhaps we'll have to wait for old Ben to pop back to give us the answer.

As the stories show many people do like visits from deceased family members though they may not broadcast it at the corner shop. But it's as well to remember that not everyone is pleased to see relatives who have gone before. Andrea who lives in Portsmouth told me about her Nan.

'My gran has always been very psychic. She is now in her nineties but is not at all pleased to get visits from her dead sister. So she shuts her eyes and tells her to go away. Gran says she knows her time is coming but there's life in her yet and she doesn't want her sister hovering round in anticipation.'

Chapter Four

Ghosts Give A Hand

INVISIBLE FRIENDS AND guardian angels are usually associated with children. But many adults also
believe that they are watched over and protected from
danger by a benign spirit. Connie told me that when she
was a young girl living in Liverpool a voice saved her
father's life: 'My Dad used to go to Dublin regularly as a
commercial traveller. One morning Dad was sitting at the
table at his boarding house window writing his order book
when a voice told him, "Get away from the window at
once!"

'Automatically Dad did as he was told and seconds later
the window blew in. Glass flew everywhere. There had
been an explosion at the factory opposite. But that wasn't
the last time Dad was protected.

'A few years later he was preparing to leave the hotel
having completed his business. Out of the blue a message
came asking if dad would cancel his trip home and meet
a man who wanted to see him. Dad was reluctant as the

next ferry wasn't for hours and he always caught the Friday morning ferry so he'd be home for the weekend. But he stayed. The man didn't turn up.

'Hours later our neighbour came rushing in to say the ferry had gone down. We believed dad was dead but of course dad arrived home. There were no phones in our road but he sent a telegram to say he was safe.

A friendly leprechaun, a coincidence or a guardian angel watching over the traveller and bringing him safe back to his family?

St Christopher is traditionally the Patron Saint of all travellers. With the advent of high speed motorways he has his work cut out.

Margaret told me that she was always very careful driving: 'But one day my mother and I had been to visit my father who was very ill in hospital with cancer. So I was very upset and not concentrating as we went on to the stretch of urban motorway. I must have drifted across the lanes because suddenly a voice said, sharply, "Get into the right lane at once."

'I pulled back into my own lane avoiding a collision with a car coming up fast on the outside. I knew it was my guardian angel whom I'd always felt to be with me. I'm now in my sixties but that was the only time he had to come so quickly to my aid.'

Even in the modern world the most traditional form of helper, an angel, complete with wings and golden halo, still has a place. Children see them all the time and have no problem about the concept.

Adults usually see them in times of danger or distress. Joan Jefferies who lives in Swindon, Wiltshire, told me of her visitation.

'In 1937, after the birth of my daughter, I was very ill

in a nursing home and had the feeling I was going to die. A doctor was holding my hand on one said of the bed and a nurse was on the other side. As I looked up I saw a beautiful angel in a long white robe holding out her hand to me and I felt myself going with her. Then the doctor said, "Think of your husband and the baby."

'The angel disappeared and from that moment I started to get better.'

But parents, even when they are dead, can also take on the role of a guardian angel. Dr Anthony Evans, who lives in Wiltshire, recalled: 'The year 1945 was a very sensitive one for my family. Shortly after the death of my mother in March, my sister, who lived in Birmingham and had looked after Mother for some time, had a strange experience.

'She'd left her house to go shopping. This involved a walk of 20 yards or so to a huge roundabout where an arterial road crossed the local road. The traffic was always very heavy.

'As she neared the corner she noticed a huge lorry tearing around the roundabout to her right. She felt a sudden pressure on her chest, like a push backwards and stopped in her tracks.

'At this moment a huge hubcap, metal and two feet in diameter flew off the lorry, bounced past her a few inches away and embedded itself in a tree to the garden to her left. She was very shocked and went home for a cup of tea.

'Some time later she told this story to an elderly gentleman friend who was a spiritualist and he said immediately, "That pressure on your chest was your mother holding you back from danger." '

Anthony says that had his sister continued walking she would have been badly injured if not killed by the hub cap.

Up until that time she had been highly sceptical of all things psychic.

So was it Mum? It wasn't the first time she'd been back to care of her family. In my book, *A Mother's Instincts,* I described how the young Anthony believed he was visited by his mum to check on him when he was in bed. I'm sure if I passed over I'd be floating to the school bus after my eldest son wailing, "Have you got your games kit, son?"

Maria who lives near Swindon, found her late father a willing helper when new technology foxed her. She wrote: 'I had been asked to use a new computer system at the school where I worked as secretary. Having been thrown in at the deep end and without any knowledge of the programme I felt rather scared. I was asked to enter information and left to get on with it.

'My father had died 13 years before but often I would talk to him when I needed help. Now I sat there and asked for his help again. I needed to get through three levels of the programme using menus to enter this particular piece of information. Each level was listed A to J. I went ahead and pressed the keys I thought were correct and jotted each letter down. At last I was in the correct part of the programme.

'To my surprise I looked down at the three letters I had pressed and they spelled "DAD". I always know he will look after me when I need help.'

Obviously Maria's father had been brushing up his processing skills. But it's not only parents who can lend a hand from beyond. 'Till Death Us Do Part' is only half the story. And husbands who hardly ever even put the kettle on in life suddenly turn into shining knights after death. Louisa's fiance Bob died in a road accident. But he'd taken out a huge insurance policy so Louisa had no financial problems after his death and was able to clear the mortgage on the home they were buying.

But a year later she met another man who persuaded her to use the house as security for his business and open a joint bank account. The business failed and Ken disappeared taking the contents of their joint account and Louisa's credit cards.

So Louisa went to a medium, wanting to let Bob know how sorry she was for messing up everything and to ask if he could help her. The message came back, 'For you babe, anything'. This, said Louisa, was Bob's favourite expression when he was doing his James Cagney impression.

Within a few days her boyfriend was picked up by the police on another matter. Fortunately, by then he had not had the chance to make too much of a hole in the account. The next week, out of the blue, Louisa was offered a good job and the chance to rent a cheap flat and is slowly getting back on her feet. Coincidence or a celestial James Cagney impersonator?

Louisa feels she is protected by Bob and this gives her the confidence to carry on in difficult times. That makes sense in psychological terms since if we feel loved and approved of we can often galvanise our own energies.

Dorothy was stranded in South Africa with two small children after the death of her husband, George. She was short of money and desperate to get back to England. One night she was lying in bed when George, her late husband, appeared. 'Oh, George, what am I going to do?' she cried.

He said nothing but smiled and Dorothy knew that everything would be all right. Within two months, Dorothy told me, just enough money for the fare back to England for herself and the kids came from an investment that George had made before he died. Dorothy had known nothing about this investment. She came back to Berkshire and met her second husband within a few months.

I've come across lots of widows and widowers who have been contacted by departed partners. Although after the initial visitations the deceased partner may pop into the background, he or she is usually around to give the odd reminder or bit of help. So I have no doubt as to the source of Ursula's nocturnal visitor.

She had lost her husband and three months later had an experience that, she said, swept over her like sunlight and in which she felt safe and protected. But one night she was troubled: 'I had mislaid some important papers including the deeds of my house. I needed them to claim an important grant. I searched all round in vain and as I lay in bed I know I said aloud, "Wherever did I put those papers?" '

We can almost hear Ursula's hubby toppling off his cloud in exasperation and shouting to any passing seraphim: 'I told her to keep them at the bank but would she listen?'

But the answer was at hand. 'At that moment I heard a voice in my ear, "They are down the back of the dressing table drawer."

'I got up at once and took the drawer right out — I'd checked the drawer earlier and discovered nothing. But they had indeed fallen down the back.'

Another case of hubby looking after his widow's interests was related to me by June of Bracknell. 'After my husband passed away we had to sell his car. I was out at the front of the house with my daughter and we could feel my husband watching us from the bedroom window. He was telling us not to be conned and to be careful with the sale. The woman who was buying the car had three young children and went off with my daughter leaving the children with me.

'They wanted to go to the toilet so I took them upstairs and as we passed my bedroom door the little girl said: "Who is that man in your bedroom?"

'I said there was no one in there but she insisted that there was.'

It is easy to imagine a husband fretting as his car is being sold but June told me that she has felt her husband taking care of her and her daughter on other occasions.

'He was a jack of all trades and dealt with all the practical matters. There was a fence at the bottom of our garden that got broken in the wind after he died. I was standing looking at it not knowing what to do. My daughter went up to the bathroom. When she came back she said: "Dad says look at the deeds before you do anything."

'On the deeds there was a mark showing where the fence should be so I took them along to the Citizen's Advice Bureau. It turned out it was council property at the back of our house and the council was liable for the damage.

'I go to his grave but I don't feel him there. He's in the house and it feels very safe. During the first few months I dreamt about him three times. But although I could feel his presence strongly in my dreams, I could not see him and this worried me. Then I had a fourth dream. He looked me full in the face and I could see him and he told me I must pull myself together and get on with life. It was so real.'

But her late husband's help does not stop with practical matters.

'Several years ago,' said June, 'my daughter and I had some bad experiences. I had gone to bed early one days as I wasn't feeling well and my husband was downstairs.

Suddenly I felt a hand over my mouth trying to suffocate me. I could feel the fingers pressing down as I was trying to breathe. Then I broke free and started to scream. My husband came rushing up and said I was dreaming, but I know I wasn't.

'Not long after that my daughter was washing her hair. She used to put her head underneath the tap as she didn't like using the shower. She felt her head being pushed underneath the water, someone was trying to drown her.

'We felt this presence around but after my husband died it stopped.'

It's nice to think of June's husband going wherever ghosts congregate and approaching some unpleasant spectre in the same way he would have had a quiet word with any other neighbourhood thug and telling him to get out of town fast.

But your guardian angel need not be a relative, or indeed, anyone remotely connected with you. Derek was a soldier but his spirit guide wasn't another military man, though he'd seen his share of fighting. Derek had been home on leave to see his mum on the Isle of Wight.

Angela, Derek's mother explained: 'Derek had a North American Indian guide from childhood that he always called Mate. Derek was due to meet a friend Tim at Folkestone Station so they could travel back to Germany together in Derek's car. But as it was Whitsun Bank Holiday, Derek got to the port at Yarmouth and found he couldn't get a ferry off the island for hours because he hadn't booked. So he decided to drive round the Island to East Cowes to try another ferry port.

'He phoned me from East Cowes where he'd still got a wait to ask me to phone Folkestone station and tell the other lad he'd be really late so to go for a meal and a wander round.

'But I hadn't realised there were two stations at Folkestone and when I rang through to the one in the town, the clerk was very rude and said if I didn't know which station the guy was at he couldn't help. But I knew I must try to get a message through as Derek would be several hours late. Derek wasn't due to phone me again till he got back to Germany.

'Then I had an idea. I went quietly upstairs and called Mate. I felt a bit daft but I said, "Look, Mate I need to get in touch with Derek. Could you get him to ring me?"

'About 20 minutes later the phone rang. "Whatever do you want, Mother?" Derek was cross. "I've been getting in and out of the car for the last 20 minutes because I knew you wanted me but I didn't have time to stop or I'd be even later with all the traffic. So make it fast."

'So I was able to ring Folkestone Harbour station where Tim was waiting and Tim went for a meal and had a wander round the town and was able to settle down for a sleep till Derek finally arrived. Tim was very grateful and they travelled the rest of the way to Germany uneventfully.

'Mate had helped Derek out before. When Derek had his motor bike, Mate would ride on the back. One morning Derek set off after leave but when he got to the ferry port Mate said, "You're not going on this boat."

' "I am," said Derek.

' "No you're not," replied Mate. "You've got to go home. You've left something important behind." He wouldn't say what. Mate liked playing games.

'Derek turned the bike round and came back completely puzzled as he thought he'd double-checked everything. But when he went upstairs he discovered all his

65

army papers on his dressing table.'

Derek wasn't a Spiritualist — he just kept his childhood friend into adulthood. But Spiritualists believe firmly we all have spirit guides and when Hilda, who lives in Manchester, joined a development circle at the local spiritualist church, she discovered that her spirit guide had hidden talents. 'When I went for the first time the leader told me to stand up and say whatever came to me. I was reluctant but the leader insisted.

'I sang, *O Worship the King.* I was surprised because I didn't have much of a voice and certainly had never wanted to sing in public before. But the voice that emerged was a strong rich one, not mine at all.

' "Oh, that was Sarah coming through," said the leader. "She was in the Salvation Army before she died and was one of their best voices."

'I was amazed but have had visits from Sarah since when singing in church. But it doesn't always happen and while I feel quite proud when this beautiful voice emerges from me, I feel deflated when it doesn't.'

Hilda concludes that you must not get too pleased with yourself as the spirits will bring you down if they think that you are getting above yourself.

Phantoms can pass on other talents which can be even more useful than singing, as this story from Pauline shows. 'My mum died when I was three and my dad couldn't cope so I was sent to live with my mother's sister. Aunty Elizabeth couldn't, she admits, thread a needle whereas my mother was a brilliant seamstress. But as soon as I went to live with my aunt she discovered that she could sew anything and made all my clothes which were really lovely. Then when I was twelve, my mother appeared to her and said, "You've made some lovely things for Pauline but now you deserve a rest." After that she never sewed again.'

Are the spirits always helpful? Maybe and maybe not. Jan, a social worker in Reading, Berkshire, told me: 'When I was eighteen I was training as a nurse. One night my friend Margaret and I were fooling around with a couple of the other nurses having a seance using a glass. We got the fright of our lives because we got in touch with a spirit who claimed to be my guide. He said his name was Melcombe Blake and that he had been a master carpenter. We said we didn't believe him so he told me the name of my mum and grandma which no one else in the room knew.

'But I thought it might be telepathy so I demanded to know something that hadn't happened yet. "Tell us the winner of the 3.30 at Sandown Park tomorrow," I asked. None of us knew anything about horse racing and that was the only racecourse name I knew.

' "Gay Trip," he told us.

'So next day we looked in the paper and there was a horse called that so we went into a betting shop, giggling like mad because we'd never been before and I thought it was one of the others having me on because this horse was an outsider. But it won and we made quite a bit of money.

'That night we called up Melcombe again. He was livid and threatened not to tell us anything else if we abused his trust.

'But we begged him and he told us that in the television programme *Going for a Song* in a month's time there would be a large round wooden table he had made. He described every detail so we couldn't mistake it and said it had been made in the early eighteenth century.

'Melcombe said he couldn't remember now the exact

67

date he'd made it but it was the day his wife Ellen was dying. He told us that the antiques expert Arthur Negus would say. "The only problem is we can't find the maker of the table."

'On the Friday there was an unexpected programme change and the programme was shown the following Sunday afternoon. The table was there and Arthur Negus said, "We cannot identify the craftsman who made it." It was the table down to the last detail.

'So I believed Melcombe after that. He told me I would marry a man with a foreign name. Since I was madly in love with a French guy it was odds on that I would marry a foreigner. But Melcombe insisted it wasn't the Frenchman but somewhere further away.

'Shortly afterwards my romance broke up and I met my husband who came from the Ukraine.

'We stopped having seances after that. Life was too full. But I often wonder if Melcombe was my guide as he said?'

It may be that Jan did get in touch with a friendly spirit. But from my own research I have found that guides very rarely emerge through seances, although sometimes a reliable medium will confirm the presence of a guide we've had from childhood. But like any friendship if it's all one-sided for gain then it rarely develops.

Melcombe was merely a party trick to Jan and her friends and perhaps if they had continued summoning him things might have turned nastier. In any event if we use psychic information purely for gain then it tends to dry up.

Rosemary, whom I met at a talk in Swindon, told me that when her father was a young man, he would be given tips on the horses by a spirit guide. These he put bets on and made more and more money. Finally he got greedy and put the lot on a winner he'd been given by this helping spirit. The horse lost and her father lost everything as a result. Rosemary commented:

'I firmly believe that if we use psychic help for personal gain then it will be taken from us. And that's exactly what happened in my father's case.'

With all psychic matters, we can come to rely too heavily on our guides and opt out of personal responsibility for our own lives. If our resident guide is consulted on every issue, then it's all too easy to wait for our mediaeval nun, or Chinese doctor, or tame Amazon to come to our aid rather than swimming for the shore ourselves.

Jennifer was told at a psychic fair that she had a gypsy woman with her who could always be relied on to come to her aid and whom she should consult at all times. After that it seemed as if Meg Merilees was indeed delivering the goods.

She was especially hot on travel and a couple of times she warned Jennifer that there would be a delay in her morning train or that clients at work would turn up late. And, in spite of a couple of near-misses when trains weren't quite as late as Meg foretold, Jennifer came to rely on Meg to keep her one step ahead.

But gradually Jennifer began consulting Meg about everything — where she should go, who she should see, what she should do — and it seemed there were more and more 'gypsy's warnings'. So when it was time for Jennifer to go on a package tour to Greece with some friends from the office, naturally she consulted Meg. Now it's bad enough listening to flesh and blood alarmists and when Meg warned her the plane would crash then Jennifer didn't hesitate. She cancelled the flight and paid a lot more for another one because the charter was one of the perks of the cheap holiday.

The charter flight didn't crash and the scheduled one was delayed due to an air traffic controllers' dispute. Jennifer lost two days of her holiday and a lot of her spending money. Obviously Meg Merilees lived before the age of the plane.

I'm not saying we should ignore our predictive abilities, nor distrust our spirit guides, but we've got to be sure that we aren't just responding to someone else's fantasy figure they've projected on to us. Probably Jennifer always had a strong inner voice that warned her about travel hazards, etc.

But when she thought about it, Jennifer realised that somehow she had always known about late trains before the arrival of Meg. In fact, Meg probably got in the way because Jennifer stopped trusting her own instincts.

Had Jennifer asked herself if she felt alarm about the plane, she might have realised that it was only normal free-floating anxiety. Often people who trust their own predictive powers have a low everyday anxiety level because they are confident that they will know a real emergency when one crops up.

If we hear an urgent voice or feel ourselves being pulled back we should go along with the call. It may be some elderly relative watching over us as she did when we were a child. Or it may be a benign spirit. But we should not allow others to attribute guides to us that we don't feel ourselves. I personally have enough spirit guides to fill Wembley Stadium, if the assurances from all the clairvoyants I've met are to be believed.

Above all, we cannot opt out of decision-making or taking normal safety precautions and hope that Aunty will leap from her cloud to catch us before we fall. The day that we take one risk too many might just be our guardian angel's day off.

I said at the beginning that this was a down-to-earth book and that angels don't just fly round saving lives and dispensing wisdom. But there are times when they can help an old lady in distress in a very practical fashion. Andrea of Portsmouth explained how her elderly gran had become very upset at the idea of her dearly departed sister hovering round her bedside. However, Andrea also recalled:

'My other gran wasn't psychic at all. But the week before she died a really strange thing happened. She was completely bedridden and my aunt had to struggle to help her to the commode. But one morning the old lady had already used it and was back in bed looking quite alert when my aunt went in to get her up. "Oh the angels came to help me and then they put me back to bed," the old lady explained to her puzzled daughter.

'Aunty thought she was rambling but the same week my gran died unexpectedly. Before she died she told my aunt she could hear beautiful music and all the nuns and priests were singing. Nan took someone's hand as she died and was smiling but my aunt could see no one. But she'd never been at all religious in her life.'

Chapter Five

Cheaper Than BT

TELEPATHY IS PERHAPS the most common psy
chic phenomenon. Most of us can recall an incident
where we've telephoned Mum or best friend to find she is
trying to dial our number. Or perhaps we have sensed the
distress of someone we care for even if he or she lives
miles away. It may be that telepathy is a natural human
ability that has fallen into disuse with sophisticated communication systems. In ancient times, how else would Mrs
Caveman have let hubby know his dinosaur stew was
ready? At its most dramatic, telepathy can be a lifesaver.

Norah, who lives in Reading, had waited almost 20
years for a child and when she got pregnant on her
twentieth wedding anniversary she was absolutely de-
lighted. Norah used to put the baby to bed in her room in
the evening so the infant wouldn't be disturbed while she
watched television downstairs. But one evening, when the

baby was a few months old, Norah suddenly felt she had to rush to the baby though she had heard nothing. When she reached the bedroom she discovered the infant had stopped breathing and was turning blue.

Norah revived the baby and took her to hospital. No cause could be found for the incident and she never before or since experienced such panic which she said was very different from normal maternal anxiety. This story was told to me by Norah's sister as we pushed our buggies home together from the local playgroup on a housing estate near Reading.

Of course it's often argued that mothers in such cases hear some unusual sound. But in my book *A Mother's Instincts,* women from all over the world recount how they saved a child's life by sensing imminent danger even when they were miles away. In one case the mother was seven miles from home in a cinema when she smelled burning and insisted on dragging her sceptical husband home on public transport.

As they reached the house which was set on its own, they saw smoke pouring under the door. The babysitter had fallen asleep and her lighted cigarette had dropped down the side of a chair. Mothers of small children seem to have an automatic radar to warn them of a child's impending danger.

Why it works in some cases to save a child's life and yet, in other cases equally loving parents don't get a chance, I don't know. All we can do is seize the chance, if we are given it.

Elaine, who lives in Reading, believes telepathic communication twice helped her to save her husband's life. She told me: 'About 16 years ago my husband Gavin had gone for the evening to an Irish Club in North London. It got very late and he phoned to say he was just leaving. By two in the morning, he hadn't arrived home and I was getting frantic. There were three pictures on the wall and at 2.10 precisely — I looked at the clock as it happened — they fell off the wall, one after the other. I grabbed my rosary beads and said the rosary. At 4.30 just as I was phoning the police, Gavin walked in the gate and said, "Elaine, I've been in an accident."

'He had crashed the car at 2.10. He had gone to sleep at the wheel, had hit the car in front and turned over. But he had emerged unscathed though the car was totally wrecked. I believe it was my prayer at that precise moment that had been answered and saved his life.'

The second incident is one more usually associated with crisis telepathy when we know someone we love is in danger and we psychically go to their aid. The earlier experiences occur when the distance is too far for physical intervention and we have to resort to psychic means.

'On another occasion I was in Mass with the children one Sunday evening when I knew we had to go home at once,' Elaine said. 'Gavin needed me. I had never left Mass early in my whole life. It was unthinkable. But I just knew it was a matter of life and death. As we arrived home, Gavin was walking out of the door.

'He said that about half an hour earlier, the time I'd left Mass everything had suddenly got too much and he had decided to throw himself off the local railway bridge. Whether he would have done so, I don't know, but a minute later I would have missed him.'

So the message is that if you feel a loved one's distress and cannot reach them physically send your love and strength and you may move mountains. But if you can go, don't hesitate. At worst you'll appear over anxious, at best

74

you could save a life.

Hayley West, who lives in Freshwater on the Isle of Wight, knew that her nan had died though Nan lived a couple of hundred miles away. 'My nan and I were always very close though she lived miles away in Derby. She was like a second mother to me. One day I'd gone up on the Downs near Ventnor with my boyfriend on his motor bike. It was a lovely day but suddenly I had the most terrible feeling and knew I had to get home as fast as possible. I felt really ill and totally frightened.

'When we reached Freshwater three different people told me my mum was very upset and was looking for me. Nan had suddenly died at the time I first had the feeling and the message had just reached Mum.'

But that wasn't Hayley's only telepathic communication. Twins often share each other's pains — I heard of one who shared her sister's labour pains though they were hundreds of miles apart. But even when the sisters aren't twins they can empathise so deeply that they share physical symptoms. Hayley told me how she linked in with her younger sister who was living in Orlando in the United States.

'Kelly and I have always been close. One day I was very ill with violent stomach pains and I was rushed to hospital with a suspected ectoptic pregnancy. At the same time my sister experienced the most dreadful stomach pains and knew it was me. Straight away she phoned my mum to see what had happened. Mum hadn't wanted to worry her.' Telepathic communication between sisters need not work only in crisis as Anne Burbidge of Leicester and her sister Eileen found. Eileen lives in Derby and recently came to stay. Anne had decided to buy some new wallpaper and showed Eileen a sample of the paper and border.

'I asked if she liked it,' said Anne. 'She replied that she liked it so much that she and her husband had just put up the same design in their house. It was a style neither of us had used before. We both chose the wallpaper because we wanted to break away from our usual style. I chose another wallpaper after that.

'So many times we have bought the same birthday cards and presents for people that it is a family joke.'

Hayley's mum hadn't wanted to worry her sister by telling her that Hayley was in hospital, But telepathic knowledge can't be concealed even for the best motives.

Julie Grist who lives in Ryde on the Isle of Wight believes she shared her mother's last moments even though the news was kept from her. 'My son was born on July 18 in hospital and my mum sent a card with a note in it congratulating me and saying she was coming to see me the next day. I was in hospital in Kent and Mum lived in Enfield. I cleared my locker that night as I was due to go home in the morning and thought I'd put the note back in the card to take home.

'I was having a shower in the evening before dinner when I slipped and fell very heavily. Because I had fallen so badly, a doctor was called.

'But the worst thing was that I was in such a state mentally afterwards, although there was no damage. I was frantic to find mum's note and went through the dustbin sack in the ward, even tipping the contents on the floor to try to find it. When my husband came he tried to calm me down, saying it didn't matter and it was only a note and I'd soon be seeing Mum. He even helped me search the bin again but it was no use. It was gone and I was inconsolable about the letter.

'Late that evening when I was alone, I just sat in the

nursery holding the baby in my arms and rocking him in my arms, crying and crying.

'A nurse said I was suffering from the baby moody blues, but I had nothing like it when my daughter was born and it was the worst feeling I had ever experienced.

'My husband came early the next morning for me and broke the news. At the time I had fallen in the shower, my mother had had a heart attack and fallen and died in her bathroom. At the time I had been holding the baby and crying, the police had arrived at my door to break the news to my husband. When I spoke to my sister she confirmed the time I had fallen and mum had died were the same.

'Two days later after I came home I had shut myself in the bathroom to have a good howl. I felt my mother's hand on my head quite gently but firmly as though she were reaching out to comfort me.

'It felt wonderful and reassured me Mum was still with me and though the pain was still bad I knew she could still reach me with her love. It was the only physical contact I ever had after her death'.

In all these cases someone tried to hold back the bad news for the very best motives but failed because the telepathic message was so strong But sometimes the concealment isn't deliberate. The person who is in danger may be blissfully unaware you are sharing his experience and what is more, if he hasn't been alerted to the hazard, he won't even be worried. Instead, you are panicking on his behalf.

I felt very uneasy on the evening of November 15, 1992, and sat by the phone till very late debating whether to ring my husband John at *The Daily Telegraph* where he works. I knew what I wanted to tell him. 'The bike is at the entrance but don't go to it.'

This was not exactly a coherent message, especially since John used the underground car park at work. So if I sent it, he might think that I'd been at the cooking sherry.

Eventually I went to bed and woke about midnight to find John standing beside the bed. What a relief he was home safe though I hadn't been expecting him. But then he disappeared. By this time I was really panicking, given the number of deathbed visions I had researched when the would-be departed appears to a loved one at the moment of his death. I went downstairs to phone his office though I knew his shift would have finished. But what could I say? 'Could you check if my husband has keeled over on his bike at the entrance to the building?'

I passed a restless night and eventually I got up at the crack of dawn to join my insomniac middle son, Jack, who was watching the early morning cartoons. I was hardly listening when the TV news came on. The newsreader announced that an IRA bomb had been discovered outside my husband's office the previous evening and had been defused. The area was at last declared safe.

At last my feelings made sense. Although, of course, it wasn't John's bike but the van containing the bomb that was outside the entrance. But my panic wasn't over. I knew that John, valuing his bike as if it was a member of the family, might well have tried to go to it and got involved in the trouble. Was that why he had not contacted me? Was he being held as a secret hostage? When finally he rang cheerfully at 10am, having overslept and forgotten to contact me, they were not words of love that hummed down the telephone wires.

Ironically, I had picked up telepathically on his danger, not his fears. My husband was working twelve storeys up at Canary Wharf in Canada Tower, which is made almost entirely of glass. Had the bomb exploded, police believe that everyone inside his office would have been slashed to death by flying glass. He and his colleagues would have stood no chance.

Yet John had experienced very little panic about the bomb during the evacuation because he and everyone else believed it was a hoax. Even when it turned out that there was a bomb outside the office, his feeling was not fear but annoyance that the front page of the paper had not been finished. So he and his friends went down to their local pub for a pint. I was the one worrying on his behalf to a potential disaster that, consciously, I knew nothing about.

So if you are in a bomb scare or other potentially hairy situation even if the media isn't splashing it across the front page, ring home as your other half may be living through every minute by proxy.

John had finally told me he was safe the day after the emergency. But then he'd reasoned nothing had actually happened. Even when faced with a real disaster the last thing you may think of doing is getting out your address book and ringing all your friends, in case they were having a psychic wobbly on your behalf.

Edwina, a solicitor from Fareham, in Hampshire, told me: 'My friend Clive went to South Africa in 1973 to work in a gold mine. One day I was suddenly very worried. It was as though everything in front of me went black. It was like being trapped in a mine, or a shutter coming down on me. I felt cold and frightened and I knew the sensation was connected with Clive and he was in danger. After about half an hour I switched on the radio — I don't know what I expected to hear — and listened to the news. The bulletin said there had been an accident in a gold mine outside Johannesburg in which five people had been killed.

79

'Although the name of the mine wasn't given and so I didn't know for sure it was Clive's I still had this dreadful feeling and so I said, "Are you all right, Clive? If you are, please let me know."

'It took half an hour before the phone rang — but then I suppose I was communicating half way across the world. It was Clive telling me the accident had been at his mine but that he had escaped unhurt. I told him the time I had the feeling and that was the exact time the accident had happened.'

Cynics will say that Clive would have phoned anyway to reassure his friend. But though he and Edwina were good friends he had many other friends in England whom he didn't contact. And Edwina did better on the psychic phone link than I did.

Many calls for help aren't life or death but occur when a friend or relation is sad or worried or has had a minor accident but does not want to bother you. Mothers and daughters are prime candidates for sharing each others woes by psychic link. Usually such bonds occur in a relationship that is loving but not possessive.

I was buying crisps for my children's packed lunch when the lady behind the counter at my local shop told me the following story; 'My daughter lives a hundred miles away in Plymouth and is married with kids but we've always been very close. One morning I couldn't stop worrying about her though we'd spoken on the phone a couple of nights before and everything was fine. At last I gave in and phoned. I said, "Look tell me to mind my own business, Faye, but is everything all right?"

' "Oh, mum," she said, "I've just found out I'm pregnant again."

'So we had a chat and she was pleased and I was

pleased. It was just a bit unexpected and she wasn't sure how I'd react.

'Another time, I was worried about my daughter and my foot started to hurt. I didn't want to bother Faye if everything was all right. So I rang her mum-in-law who lived in Plymouth near her and asked if Faye was OK.

' "Well she fell downstairs this morning and hurt her foot . She's been to hospital but nothing's broken so she didn't want to worry you." '

As I said, you can sometimes get more worried if the person concerned doesn't get in touch, so it's important to get the earthly communication going swiftly, if hearts and psyches are beating as one.

Sometimes psychic communication can be a tangible expression of caring and break the ice where a problem is hard to share. I was at a psychic fair in London when I met Joy, a middle-aged woman from Wandsworth. She described how she suddenly felt very worried about Trish, a friend she hadn't seen for a few weeks.

'I had a very vivid dream in which I phoned my friend and she was very distressed but she wouldn't tell me what was wrong. So she decided to telephone to see if anything was wrong. Trish is Jewish and always very cheerful, but the dream was so vivid I did ring her the next evening to tell her about it, though it seemed silly, and to ask if there was a problem. Trish assured me she was fine but she sounded a bit strange.

'But the next day a letter came from Trish. She explained that when I'd phoned her father was in the room so she couldn't talk but she'd very recently found a lump in her breast and hadn't felt able to tell anyone. My phoning and sounding concerned had broken the ice. She was so glad to be able to tell someone.'

The moral seems to be that if you do feel instinctively a friend needs you then contact them. At the worst they'll think you're fussing, but you may be there when they need support but can't ask.

Mainly the cases come from women perhaps because men find it harder to tell such tales. But Frank who lives in Stockport told me how he linked with his elder married daughter through dreams: 'Gillian lived some miles distant and we didn't see a great deal of her or her husband. But he seemed a nice enough chap and when we got together it was always a very happy occasion. But then I started to have a series of dreams in which my daughter came to me and was crying on my shoulder and saying. "Daddy, you have no idea."

'I comforted her in the dreams but they were so vivid that I did try to broach the subject when we next met but she insisted everything was fine. But the dreams continued and one day my daughter arrived home saying she'd left her husband and that he had hurt her many times.

' "Daddy you have no idea," she said.

'And so I told her of the dreams and I think it helped her to trust me. It wasn't easy but we got through the crisis and she's now happily remarried.'

Fascinating though crisis telepathy is, the vast majority of such communication is more mundane. Husbands and wives frequently report everyday telepathic links —— if they notice them. For most pass in the to-ing and fro-ing of everyday life and it's only when asked that we become aware of an almost daily unspoken conversation. The existence of such routine telepathy isn't surprising since telepathy seems strongest between those who have an emotional bond.

But this makes it hard to measure. The card guessing

experiments in a laboratory can't even begin to encounter the human element. Telepathy then is primarily a link of love. And for every life and death experience there are a hundred everyday communications that simply affirm that affection and caring doesn't operate within the bounds of time and space. And if we can trust these instincts then they can save us time and effort.

Constance was waiting at the barrier at Heathrow Airport when Gordon arrived on the morning flight from Geneva where he'd been on business for several days.

'How did you know I'd be coming on this flight?' he asked. 'I was going to surprise you.'

Usually it is the female of the species who has the flashes of insight, not because women are more psychic but perhaps because they find it easier to rely on such insights. Or it may be that women are more used to thinking on behalf of their families. I know that with my five kids I have to fine-tune arrangements down to the last non-matching sock. And the normal just extends a bit further into what is sometimes called paranormal.

As I said, this book is about the stuff of everyday living that the soap operas would dismiss as dull, because it's at this grass root level that real magic goes about its business almost unnoticed.

One advantage (or disadvantage,depending on your position) in marital telepathy is that it's an excellent way of keeping tabs on a partner. Grace, who lives in Liverpool, told me that her husband was a travelling salesman who would never know which of several areas he would be sent to when he left home in the morning. But if she needed to contact him to bring a loaf home or find out what time he'd be back she didn't bother to ring the office to trace his whereabouts. A call would come through wherever he was supping his lunchtime or evening pint

'I was never wrong,' Grace told me: 'In fact, he was terrified to chat up a pretty barmaid in case I arrived on my broomstick!' Grace is not alone in her psychic monitoring.

Mike, who lives in Harrow, told me how one evening he had stopped on the way home from work for a quick drink with a friend, Barry, whom he'd bumped into in London while getting off the tube. Mike hadn't seen Barry for years because his wife Julie didn't like Barry as she thought he would lead Mike off the straight and narrow. When Mike got home, Julie was waiting. His excuses about the delays at work and the missed trains dried up as if by magic when she said: 'Don't tell me lies. You've been drinking with that Barry.'

Mike wasn't surprised by his wife's magical powers. His own parents ran a shop when he was a child and his mum would always send telepathic messages to Dad if she needed a loaf or some cheese bringing home. 'It worked every time,' Mike told me. 'The annoying thing is neither Dad nor I could do it back.'

Very occasionally it seems that we can pick up strong emotions not connected with us and find ourselves wanting to behave totally out of character. Sam Larkin who is an actor and lives just about everywhere told me about his free floating telepathy:

'I am a very peace-loving person but one day I passed a man and had a strong urge to bring him down in a rugby tackle and then punch his face in. This anger shocked me and I felt very guilty though I did nothing. As I turned the corner I saw a woman lying on the pavement and two other women trying to comfort her. She had been mugged and badly assaulted by the man I had passed.'

I would not suggest you use Sam's intuition as a defence in court if you happened to wreak vengeance on the wrong passer-by. But his experience does add to the evidence that telepathy is driven by feeling. It also suggests that it's not just a fallacy that if we think positively (or negatively), we can influence the world around us.

But all telepathy isn't so purpose driven. On occasions it seems we just flit into the mind of a friend or acquaintance and pick up a random thought, which can be a bit embarrassing. Danielle who lives in Crewe described: 'I was at breakfast with a friend, just the two of us. And as I looked at her mouth as she spoke the thought came from nowhere into my head, "She has a mouth like a hen's bottom."

'I nearly laughed out loud, But immediately she said, "My brother Sammy says I have a mouth like a hen's bottom."

'Needless to say I didn't enlighten her as to our telepathic bond.'

Chapter Six

A Tip For The 3.30

PREMONITIONS, LIKE TELEPATHY, can be life-savers if we react promptly. The major difference is that with premonition the warning comes of future danger or distress, while telepathy picks us problems as they happen and we may only have seconds or minutes to prevent the danger escalating to disaster.

No one really understands the hows or whys of premonitions, but in some cases we are given the chance to save our loved ones. What have we to lose? Such links are common between mother and child and the mother seems to act as an early warning system until the child gets a sense of danger for himself.

Perhaps this is one of the surviving manifestations of this ancient instinct because it serves a real need. Telepathy and premonition tend to overlap in this area because the time difference may be very small and it's hard to tell, for an example, whether a mother has a vision of a choking baby seconds before it happens and reaches him as the premonition becomes reality, or whether she detects his distress as it begins and then reacts. In practice you just go and don't stop to argue about the mechanics.

Gloria, who lives in Bournemouth, is now in her late sixties. But she recalled that as a young mother she suddenly heard a voice saying urgently: 'Go to the railway line quickly. The children are in danger.'

'I rushed automatically to the railway though the children never played there. But this day they had climbed over the fence and were playing on the track. It was in the days of pre-electrification and, mercifully, I got there just in time.'

Only afterwards did Gloria realise there had been no one present at the time of the warning and that there was no special reason the children should be at the railway, rather than in the safe places where they normally played. Many adults, not just mothers, have this protective power if they trust themselves. And as with telepathy love is strongly implicated.

Often it is a family member or a close friend that is involved in the premonition. Far more people have premonitions about family or friends than about international disasters, though it is the more spectacular global experiences that hit the headlines.

But where national calamities can rarely if ever be prevented, familial forewarnings can sometimes offer a chance to save those we love. The warning may be heard as a voice, as an inner gut feeling, or pictorially in a dream or vision. But the quality of the experience is very different from normal anxiety.

Elspeth from Fareham, has found on more than one occasion that listening to her premonitions did save lives. In *A Mother's Instincts,* I described how five-year-old

87

Elspeth had warned her mum during the Second World War that a bad plane was coming. The sky was clear and her mother was reluctant to obey her daughter.

But seconds later a bomber came from behind a cloud and sprayed the beach with bullets. Elspeth explained her foreknowledge was a family gift. But it may be that because she accepted predictive powers as natural she used them automatically to avoid life's pitfalls.

'As a child I always knew that Dad knew things before they happened. If Dad said something would happen, I just accepted it as a fact. I could foretell things so I believed everyone could do it. I was surprised at junior school when I found other people couldn't predict what was going to happen. When I told people I found they were laughing at me or dismissed me as odd.

'As an adult, I still generally keep quite about my foreknowledge unless it's life or death. One male friend was very sceptical of psychic matters until we went to South Wales together. It was early one morning and very foggy. "Colin, pull over," I shouted suddenly. "There's a car coming on the wrong side of the road!"

' "No, I've got my headlights on and I can't see anything," he replied.

' "Pull over now," I insisted and, sensing the urgency in my voice, he did. You could hardly see the width of the road the fog was so bad. A Land Rover with no lights came hurtling round the bend on the wrong side of the road. Had we not pulled over at that moment he would have hit us head on. The strange thing was that I hadn't even been looking at the road when I spoke.

' "I'll never doubt you again," he said. Now he automatically pulls over if I tell him to and his no-claims bonus is intact.'

Wheels and premonitions seem to go together because once you graduate from your trike in the back yard the world can be a pretty dangerous place when viewed at speed. Elspeth's friend responded to the urgency in her voice but it isn't always that simple. How can we convince others we're not off our trolley if, out of the blue, we prophesy disaster?

Like Cassandra, my namesake in the Greek legend, we are unlikely to be believed. Carole explained how listening to her inner voice saved her life but that she didn't speak out to warn her family because she knew they would only mock her.

'We were living in Slough. One Sunday my mum, dad, brother and I were planning to visit my gran who had a flat in Uxbridge. I was a teacher and on alternate Sundays I used to take a party of kids to an old people's home. This Sunday, I'd told the kids I couldn't go. But as I started to open the car door a voice said to me, "Don't get in the car. You'll never see it again."

'I don't know what I said to Mum and Dad. I just knew I couldn't get in the car or I would die. But I couldn't warn them. They'd got impatient on other occasions when I'd known things in advance. They'd have said, as usual, that I was being stupid and that it was my imagination. Besides, somehow I knew that it was only me who would die. But afterwards I felt so guilty that I hadn't at least tried to make them listen.

'Instead of going to see my gran, I ended up at the old people's home with the kids. But all afternoon I felt in a dream and hurried home as fast as possible. As I walked up the path of my house I heard the phone ringing and I knew. It was the local hospital. The car had been hit by a tall lorry and the roof had caved in on the back seat. The only thing that had saved my brother was the fact he had been lying flat across the back seat — he always went to sleep on journeys if he had the back seat to himself.

'The police said that had there been two people sitting in the back of the car they would have been decapitated.

'I know I couldn't have prevented the accident. But because I hadn't gone in the car, my brother was only badly shocked.'

But premonitions bring no guarantees. Time and again I am asked by people who tell me their stories why they weren't given the opportunity to save a child or husband. There appear to be no reasons behind premonitions and sometimes little consolation.

However, other people say they have appreciated the chance to make the most of the time. Phyllis, who lives in Rayleigh in Essex, told how an advance message of comfort gave her the strength to cope.

'My husband had been retired for years and we were greatly enjoying his retirement. Early in November I became restless, weepy and unable to sleep. I thought it was probably a delayed reaction to my mother's death some months previously. Having finally fallen asleep one night I was woken at exactly 6am by a cultured voice. I had a mental picture of a swirling mist coming through a lighted tunnel.

'The voice said quite clearly, "Trust in God". I was aware that all my stress had gone and the day was going to be a happy one. And it was.

'But at 7 o'clock the following morning, my husband collapsed in a massive fit followed by three others and I was aware that this was what the message was talking of. A brain tumour was diagnosed and my husband died within a few months. My husband was an atheist and so put his trust in me and I put my trust in God as the message said and somehow we found the courage to see things through to the end.

'I am a very rational and level-headed person but I am convinced the voice enabled me to cope with all the traumatic days that followed.'

Even people who are not churchgoers find in times of crisis that their faith in God resurfaces. Others believe the voice is a guardian angel or deceased relative. But what matters more than disputing the source of the voice — and we may all interpret the voice according to our personal beliefs — is that it gave Phyllis peace of mind. Phyllis felt her advance warning, however vague, helped her to face the future calmly. In some cases getting our anxious feelings over in advance does help us to be calm when crisis strikes.

Pat Gardener, who lives in a small town on the Isle of Wight, told me that one afternoon when her husband went out in the car she couldn't settle because she just knew something bad was going to happen to him. 'When he at last walked through the door, I was so relieved but he was as white as a sheet. "I've just hit a motor-cyclist," he said. "It wasn't my fault."

'Because I'd done my panicking in advance, I was able to stay calm, get him to the doctor for something to calm his nerves and sort out the police and a solicitor.'

Premonitions can also give us a chance to say goodbye. I was doing a phone-in when Jack came on the line. 'My elderly mother was ill in hospital in Portsmouth,' he told me, 'but not in any danger. One afternoon however I knew I must go and see her. When I reached the hospital, a nurse said, "You got our message then?"

'My mum had suddenly collapsed and I was there to say

goodbye.'

I could sympathise because the mother of a friend had told me a very similar story. For even encounters after death cannot fully make up for the words of love that were never spoken in life. Eileen who was living in Manchester had a severely handicapped son so visiting a sick friend was not easy.

She recalled: 'The husband of my best friend was ill with cancer and one evening his wife Flo rang to ask if we would like to go round as he was feeling down. I had had a dreadful day with my son Paul. He had fits and was very hyperactive and on his bad days he really could not be taken visiting.

'My husband who took the call asked what he should say. "Tell Flo we'll visit Alf on Saturday," I said. "We can't risk Paul like this with someone so ill."

'But as I was buttering bread for tea, a voice said, "Go today. He won't be here on Saturday."

'It didn't make sense because although Alf was obviously very ill, he wasn't expected to die for some months. "I've changed my mind," I told Bill when he came in the room.

'Flo was amazed to see us but I said it was nearly our wedding anniversary so as we were passing we'd popped in to see if they'd like to come to our party. It was stifling in the room and I was terrified about what eight-year-old Paul would do. But to my amazement he went up to Alf and said, "Would you like me to sing you some hymns?"

'Alf was really pleased and Paul sang 'Two little Eyes' which he'd learned at special school. He sang like an angel all the hymns he knew and though Alf was in pain he smiled and said, "I love that little fellow."

'I couldn't believe how beautifully Paul behaved or

how he knew all those hymns. Alf promised he'd come to the party but on the Friday he was admitted to hospital as his condition had suddenly deteriorated.

'Flo rang on Friday night and said to me, "You know what I am going to say." I replied, "Saturday would have been too late." '

Had Alf wanted to hear the little boy sing him on his way and had Paul been given some special ability for the occasion? Sometimes it is important to follow the seemingly illogical urge to say goodbye or 'I love you' or 'I'm sorry'. There is not always a tomorrow.

A social worker I know crossed Reading with a bunch of the first daffodils for her nan. It was a freezing foggy February night and the visit was totally spontaneous. When Jane got there to her nan's house, to her surprise her mother had also turned up out of the blue. Nan was full of high spirits about a Torvill and Dean show she'd seen on TV and in perfect health. But two days later she was dead. Jane is so glad she went for the last time to see her.

Esther, from Bournemouth, had a similar experience. When she was a student at teacher training college during the 1950s, the students were only allowed one weekend home a term. 'It was the first week back and suddenly I had an overwhelming feeling that I must return home the very next weekend. I went to the head of the college who tried to dissuade me from using my pass so early in the term and suggested I was just feeling homesick.

'I told her that of course I was feeling homesick but this was different. I insisted because I knew I must go home. During that weekend Dad became seriously ill and died on the Monday.'

The power to know the future is a double-edged sword and for every person who is grateful for foreknowledge comes another who really would sooner not have known what was round the corner especially if the results were inevitable.

Occasionally researchers concentrate on the proof aspects of foreknowledge and encourage would-be subjects to note down times and dates forgetting the human effects. People sometimes ring me in tears asking me how they can block knowledge of what they cannot prevent and there are no easy answers.

Although I claim absolutely no paranormal powers myself, one psychic famed for her accurate premonitions telephoned me late one night to ask me if I thought it was safe for her young grandson to travel to France as he'd had bad feelings that he wouldn't come back. So why, since she could foretell international disasters, were her powers less strong when it came to more personal issues?

Felicity, contacted me when I was doing a radio phone-in programme that covers the south-west of England. She is in her late fifties and told me that no one would believe her premonitions. What Felicity wanted to know was how she could stop them, because she felt she was somehow causing the disasters by dreaming about them.

'I dreamed my eldest son would have a car accident and fracture his skull. It was so strong I begged him not to use his car for a while — he didn't need to — but he just laughed. I had the dream three times and each time begged him but he ignored me. On the fourth night his car was involved in a collision and he fractured his skull though fortunately not badly. I feel responsible.'

Felicity had had other dreams about family members that had come true. For example, she'd known her husband was going to die and begged him to go for a check-up. He'd ignored her advice and he collapsed suddenly. I tried to suggest that at least she was prepared for disaster, but she felt that she'd lived through the anguish twice.

The real problem was that she felt she was causing the disasters. I told her that her dreams were just like a television camera recording a scene, albeit in advance. But she was distressed as she'd started dreaming about a nephew. I tried to think of ways she could shut her knowledge out, but I don't think I was a lot of help.

What if you dreamed that a family member was going to die, but you didn't know how and only that it would be soon. Would you tell the person? I don't think I would, but then I'd feel guilty, feeling that perhaps I could have prevented it.

That was the dilemma facing Margaret from Dublin. 'When I was eighteen years old I woke one morning and told my mother that Uncle Fred was going to die soon and that Daddy (who had died three years before) was coming for him. My mother was really shocked and insisted, "You were only dreaming."

'But I told her it wasn't a dream I'd had. It was a vision in my sleep. I saw lots of white clouds moving and my late father came out of them smiling and looking so happy. To my left on land I could see my Uncle Fred. My father beckoned and as Fred went towards him, my dad said, "I am taking Fred". Fred and my father smiled and waved back until they vanished into the white clouds.

'Uncle Fred was only 40 and not at all ill. But I knew when I woke up that he was going to die very soon and I told my mother that I must tell the family. She warned me not to but I insisted they must know. That was a Tuesday morning and I told the family the same day. I didn't know whether I ought to tell Uncle Fred himself but by Wednesday I decided I must. It shows how convinced I felt that I went ahead.

'I told him about the dream. He wasn't at all angry or offended. He clapped his hands, smiled and said, "There is no harm in knowing."

'On Friday night as I passed my uncle's house on my way home, the door opened and Uncle Clive ran out. "Margaret, tell your mother Uncle Fred's just collapsed. I'm going for the doctor and the priest."

'The doctor said the night would tell a lot but I knew there was no hope. Fred died two hours later from a clot to the brain.'

Should Fred have contacted a doctor? Would I want to know if someone dreamed I was on my way over? We are left with more questions than answers as usual. Margaret told her uncle of his impending death because she was convinced he had only a short time left.

But the message may be less clear and there may be no time limit. Teresa felt that the appearance of her dead brother-in-law in her husband's dream brought a warning of death, even though the words used were apparently comforting. She was so worried that she went to a medium for advice. It was Pauline, the medium who lives in Hemel Hempstead, who told me the story.

'One afternoon Teresa came to see me to ask the meaning of a dream her husband Joe had the previous night. Her husband hadn't given the dream a second thought after he had recounted it and laughed at his wife's attempts to stop him driving his beloved car that morning. Her husband had dreamed he saw his dead brother-in law, Ted. Joe was sitting in his crashed white car. Ted opened the door of the car for him and said, "Don't worry, you've come through with only a few scratches."

'I was at a loss how best to help Teresa. I said that

96

maybe her husband was worried about something. It's better to lose a bit of credibility than frighten people if you see something bad. And I did feel very strongly that all would not end happily in this case.

'But what could I advise Teresa to do short of locking the poor chap up? There was no time scale given in the dream, you see. Of course I suggested she nagged him about driving carefully and have the car checked. But I felt uneasy.

'A week later Teresa phoned to say her husband had been killed in a car crash. A supermarket lorry had collided with his car crushing him.'

While most predictions seem to concern a specific event often a death or disaster, occasionally it seems possible to catch a glimpse of a future stage of someone's life. I came across the experience of a man who had a vision of his young daughter as a woman. Of course that could be based partly on the likelihood of the child resembling another family member. But in Esme's case the glimpse she and her daughter had of Esme's husband's future was so unlikely as to be laughable.

Thirteen-year-old Susie had dreamed her father was in bed with a young dark curly-haired woman. In the dream, Susie had caught them and they were very embarrassed Esme roared with laughter when Susie told her. 'My husband was a clergyman and the most staid, unadventurous person you could imagine,' she said.

'Soon after I had a dream. In it, I went into a tumbledown cottage and saw my husband, but he was incredibly scruffy and was holding a tin of cannabis. Then the police burst in. At first I sat on the tin of cannabis and then, panicking, I threw it on to the fire.

'In the dream I knew it was a stupid thing to do but

realised I had to try to save my husband.

'Months later it all came to pass. My husband threw up his living for a young woman, moved out and ended up in appalling conditions and hooked on drugs.'

So if you dream about your partner having a fling, keep tabs on him or her, just in case. It may be your subconscious warning you that all is not well, or perhaps something more. Not all premonitions are dramatic. But all too often the more down-to-earth experiences are not told because they may seem too trivial to report. And yet these homely areas may, if pieced together, make a strong case for psychic experience as an everyday instinct that we just don't notice.

Pamela from Eastbourne, a woman in her forties whom I met at a psychic fair in London, told me of a seemingly mundane dream that came true. 'Recently I had a dream that I owned a black Manx cat though I didn't have a cat at all. Later that week a friend at work mentioned in conversation that her husband's friend had to find a new home for his cat as he was going abroad.

'Since having the dream I'd decided I'd quite like a cat so I offered to go along and see if I liked it. It was black as in my dream, but it wasn't Manx. However it didn't have a tail since it had been involved in an accident with a car and lost it. Needless to say, I took it home and now I've got my witches' cat.'

All these experiences put forward a pretty strong case for trusting your instincts. But occasionally common sense needs a hearing.

In the previous chapter I told how Elaine sensed her husband's danger when three pictures fell off the wall and she sent him her prayers which she believed saved him. But if you don't get the feeling of danger then your crashing picture could simply have a frayed cord.

Lilian Skeels told me the following tale as we sat in her mobile home not far from the executive estates of Bracknell: 'Grandad Leonard was away in the First World War. One afternoon a picture fell suddenly from the wall and Granny who greatly fancied her psychic powers took this to mean that Grandad was communicating with her telepathically with his dying breath.

'In spite of the absence of a telegram from the War Office, she accepted that he was no more. She sold the double bed and set herself up in a dressmaking business to the gentry.

'Six months later, standing at the door was the returning hero. "You're supposed to be dead," Granny told him icily. His excuse was that he just hadn't got around to writing for a few months. But Granny was not amused. Nor was Grandad when he discovered that the double bed was gone. When his leave was over, Grandad went back to the front with Granny L's optimistic words ringing in his ears, "You'll never last the War." '

He did — probably just to prove her wrong — and a new double bed was duly purchased but, as Lilian said, after that the marriage never really gelled.

Chapter Seven

A Flit Round
The Suburbs

IN THE FIRST chapter we came across the near death experience, when Doris Dunn's soul left her body and she had an astral tour of Bracknell, rather than the eternal city. But there are other types of out of body experiences, or 'oobies' as they are sometimes called, which have nothing to do with serious illness.

You can pick up cheap books or go to classes purporting to teach the correct technique to go flyabout. I would not dare to try it myself — I would be too worried about getting back into my body afterwards. Anyway, my research shows that by far the majority of oobies happen quite spontaneously. And usually they have a reason.

The Reverend Tom Willis described how his daughter's friend popped in on Christmas Day: 'My daughter Corrine was a nurse in Edinburgh and it was the first time she'd been away from home at Christmas. She was the only one of her crowd not to get Christmas Day off. A couple of days before she brought her blue duvet cover back home and changed it for an orange one.

'When she came back a couple of days after Christmas she told us of a weird experience. She woke on Christmas morning and felt someone sit on her bed. The bed went down and when she tried to move her foot she found she could not get it past a certain spot. Corrine was facing the wall but she knew no one could be in the room because the bedroom door was locked and there were bars at the window.

'As she turned the presence was gone. I suggested it might be her granny come back as she was alone on Christmas day but Corrine was sure it wasn't. Then after New Year the mystery was solved. Corrine told us that her best friend Heather who was also a nurse had told her she had a vivid dream on Christmas morning. She'd thought "Poor Corrine the only one of us on duty" and had found herself in Corrine's room sitting on the bed.

'Heather told her, "You were facing the wall and you had on your ruffled nightie. You turned round and I thought I'd better go before I frightened you. It was so real I only know it was a dream because you had an orange duvet cover and I knew yours was blue." '

Corrine and Heather did have a telepathic link, Mr Willis explained: 'When Corrine was back home in York-shire working at an old folks home much later when Heather was married, she had a strange feeling at 3.30 one afternoon and thought strongly of Heather and wondered if something was wrong.

'A fortnight later she had a letter from Heather to say she'd started to miscarry at 3.30 on the afternoon that Corrine had had the feeling. Now Heather is a mother and they've lost touch to some extent and Corrine doesn't pick things up. But such experiences are common.'

Mother love is a strong incentive for astral travel and the automatic bond can call us even when we are not aware of it on a conscious level and we go to offer comfort whether our child is three or 30. Margaret is now in her sixties and explained how some years ago she was visiting Oberammergau: 'On Sunday morning I was dressing for church when I had a strong desire to put on a navy dress and shoes and use my navy bag though I couldn't think why.

'During the service at 11 am I had the strangest tingling feeling in my legs — I've never experienced anything like it before or since. I can only describe it as a psychic feeling. The next morning we flew home and I discovered my grown-up daughter Elizabeth was very ill and about to be admitted to hospital.

'She told me, "Oh, Mummy, I felt so ill yesterday. But then at 11 o'clock, you came and stood by my bedside and I felt much better. You were wearing your navy dress, navy shoes and navy bag."

'The time I appeared to Elizabeth was when I felt that strange sensation in my legs in the church at Oberammergau. So I suppose I went to her when she needed me.'

But oobies do not have to involve contacting another person and the flight may be quite brief although extremely vivid. Nancy from Hull had an oobie while lying in bed with her husband. Cynics might say she was dreaming, but oobies, say those who have had them, tend to be a different quality from dreaming, more akin to a child floating downstairs which we only stop when we realise we shouldn't be able to do it.

Nancy explained: 'I'd spent a lovely evening with my

husband and some friends who were staying overnight at our house. We watched a film on TV and then decided to go to bed.

'My husband fell asleep almost at once. But although I was tired I couldn't settle. Suddenly I was aware of lots of small balls of light either white or pale yellow in colour which were flying at me from two corners of the room. As soon as they reached me they flew away to a large white mist at the bottom of the bed about four feet off the floor. While all this was happening I felt myself floating off my bed.

'At first I wasn't very high but I continued upwards towards an ever-growing white cloud. At this point I panicked and grabbed my husband's arm to stop myself disappearing. This seemed to do the trick and I was back in bed. My husband didn't wake up at all.'

A common feature of such experiences is that menfolk usually slumber on unaware of their wives' astral acrobatics. Oobies can be quite frightening if you don't expect one and occasionally one can come out of the blue at a time you're just relaxed. Many oobies occur either at night or in the early morning. Perhaps this is because that is when our conscious minds intrude least — it's back to the 'if you know it's impossible you don't do it'.

Tina, a young married woman, lives in Scunthorpe. She was in bed when she had her one and only oobie, apparently without reason. But as I will explain in the chapter on nasties, for a woman, the teens and early twenties can be a strange time especially for woman in establishing an identity that combines both the caring and competitive sides modern society demands: 'My husband had gone to work leaving me to have a lie in. I heard a loud buzzing noise like a dynamo in my left ear. It wasn't pleasant and I felt mystified. Then the room seemed to spin round very rapidly like a spin dryer.

'The next moment I was floating 12 inches above and to the left of my physical body still lying on the bed. My mind became crystal clear and as I looked at myself face to face, so to speak, I thought I wasn't as good looking as I had believed. Then I thought about moving up to the ceiling and in a second I was there. I wondered how to get back to my body. So I took a deep breath and I was back on the bed feeling utterly astonished and very scared.'

Oobies can also occur at a time of great stress or when the hold of the material world is at its weakest. I've discovered many women have out-of-body experiences at the time they are giving birth. They may see angels or dead relatives even when no drugs have been administered and their lives are not in danger. It is hardly surprising that women should have these Near-Birth Experiences, as I call them, and leave their bodies at such a time since, only at death do we come so close to touching another dimension.

But occasionally an out-of-body experience can occur either before or after labour, especially with a first child when what lies before a new mother can seem frightening as well as exciting.

Elizabeth, a nurse from Wells in Avon, described her out of the body experience the night before her son was born: 'My son was born in a hospital ward in Windsor on December 26, 1945. The same night I became aware of rising out of my body (very fully conscious) until I was in the upright position and drifted down till my feet were almost on the floor. I looked round at my body asleep on the bed with interest. 'There were my eyes and ears in the bed, yet I could see and hear acutely. To my amazement as my body had no weight, I didn't have to put one foot in front of the other to travel. I only had to look and wonder about going somewhere and I was gliding towards the spot.

'I looked at the door and wondered if I went out of the ward would I be able to return? Just looking at the doorknob, I found myself accelerating so fast towards it that panic took hold and it was as if a piece of elastic attached to my back, flipped me backwards into my body and suddenly I was in with it and one with it.

'I remember being disappointed afterwards that no friends were there to greet me. I thought surely at death (or at least passing to a greater life as I believe I did) there'd be a welcome from at least a guardian angel. But there were just those other patients in the ward, sleeping and unaware of me.

'I used to talk to my son before he was born and saw him as an adult who might even be an older soul than me. I felt we were on a wavelength of understanding.'

Since oobies can be nasty and are always unpredictable I wouldn't recommend you try to develop your astral side as a party trick. Concentrating on the top corner of a room, counting to a hundred or trying to hypnotise yourself and the other recommended methods of leaving your body may work, but you may find the experience frightening. If there is a need or reason for you to have an out of body experience, it will just happen without any psychic training.

Megan fancied herself as an astral traveller and went on a very expensive course in London, not at a reputable centre but a workshop organised in a North London hall. And complete with manuals, also purchased at great price, she returned home to Staines to go walkabout. Her new skills worked too well. She found she was drifting off at all sorts of inconvenient times, at the bus stop, at meetings at work and at night so she felt constantly exhausted.

At last she went back to her guru who for an even larger fee de-programmed her. Megan may have been particularly receptive or the cynics would say over-imaginative.

Near Death Experiences have been widely researched and indeed quite a few people have experienced glimpses of another world at times when their lives have been in danger. Indeed most families have one such story in their history.

But, in human terms, such experiences can lead to dilemmas and people who have had these visions may need months of help to resolve the confrontation with death.

Wendy, who is in her late forties and lives in Sheffield, described how when she was twenty five she died momentarily during an operation for a ruptured appendix.

'I remember shooting at a great speed along a black tunnel towards a point of light. When I reached the end I was floating in cotton wool clouds. I floated towards a big gold door. It swung open and there behind it stood my grandad who'd died when I was 15. "Grandad!" I cried and I hugged him.

' "You've got to go back, lass," he told me. "I want a strapping grandson to play for Sheffield United." Grandad was a great football fan.

' "But Grandad," I said, "I've split up with Rob. I'll never have children now." Rob was my ex-husband and we'd separated because he hadn't wanted children for years, if ever, while I was desperate to start a family .

' "He'll be back," Grandad promised. "Give my love to your Nan. Now be off for your tea."

'That was what Grandad used to say when I was a little girl and went to visit my grandparents. They lived in the next street and worried if I wasn't home before dark, even when I was a teenager. It sounds a strange conversation to have when you're dying but at the time it seemed quite natural.

'Then I shot back down the tunnel and woke up in a hospital bed with tubes sticking out everywhere. My ex was by my bedside crying. We did get back together for a while though we never sorted out the issue of children. But I have fostered kids with my new partner so maybe one day grandad will get his wish.'

I was told the following story by a priest that I met in Bournemouth while I was giving a lecture. He ministered to William who was elderly and dying. But William's sons, with whom he had quarrelled bitterly years before, refused to come to his death-bed. He was unconscious but to everyone's amazement he came back and said, 'I've been to the Pearly Gates. But when I got there I was told, "Not yet." '

The next morning his sons relented and came to visit him and the family was reconciled. Shortly afterwards he died.

Shakespeare told us that 'All the world's a stage'. Did he have an experience like Danielle who comes from Crewe? 'I awoke in the night having swallowed a bit of nut the wrong way. I had unwisely eaten one just before going to sleep and woke choking and coughing. The room was in pitch blackness. There appeared an audience in light clothing with hands above their shoulders applauding me, clapping soundlessly, silver lights all around them.

'I thought how absurd, how incongruous how shabby I am, how nice they are. They were so pleased with me.

Then that section of the audience was drawn aside and a much wider audience was shown. Finally that was withdrawn and a small section was shown for quite a long time of young people in front seats. I thought it all quite ludicrous at such a time with my distress.

'When I told my grandchildren about the experience they thought the people were terrible to be clapping me when I was in distress. But the audience all looked so kind and so pleased to see me though I knew none of them.'

Another strange phenomenon is when other people see the NDE rather than the person whose life is in danger. Rosemary Benham lives in Northwood on the Isle of Wight. She told me how her daughter Jane who is now twenty nearly died from whooping cough when she was 10 months old.

'As Jane lay dying in an oxygen tent in St Mary's Hospital, Portsmouth, the Sister told me all I could do was will her to live. I can see every detail all these years later, her viyella dress covered in white smocking. I can even remember the shop it came from. There was a drip in her head. Then I saw a silvery white line going from her out of the tent. It was like a piece of wool, not a bright line and not silver, not white but in between. I'd heard about the silver cord we all have but this was nothing like I imagined.

'From then a fantastic peace came over me. I thought, "Perhaps I want her too much," and I let her go and accepted what would be would be. But from then she started to get better. She was in hospital for 12 weeks. I've tried to tell people but they think I'm mad so I shut up.'

Jane is Rosemary's adopted daughter — the psychic ties are more than those of blood, based primarily on love and care. It seems that sometimes our astral bodies can be seen by others not just as lights but in our actual form. Living ghosts are a fascinating phenomenon.

The Reverend Tom Willis told me that they usually appear when someone is close to death: 'During the war people who were wounded would think of home and suddenly appear by mum's bedside. But it didn't mean they were dead — often they came back alive. Living ghosts are not uncommon.'

I had come across several experiences of this kind. Anne from Newbury, in Berkshire, told me that one night her Dad had materialised in her living room and said, 'I just wanted to tell you I'm all right, gel.'

Anne said he was wearing smart fawn slacks and a fawn sweater. 'Then before I could say anything he disappeared. Since Dad lives thousands of miles away in Australia I reasoned he must be dead. I'd heard of people coming across the world to say goodbye. But no phone call came from Mum and so I didn't know what to do. After all I could hardly ring up and ask if Dad was dead. But after two days I could stand the waiting no more and phoned to ask how Dad was.

' "How did you know something was wrong?" she asked because we had regular days for phoning as it was expensive. She explained Dad had been taken ill and rushed to hospital for an emergency operation. She hadn't wanted to worry me as he was all right now. When I questioned her she explained he had momentarily died during the operation. Given the date difference it had been the time I had seen dad in my living room. I asked her what he had been wearing when he was admitted to hospital. It was no surprise when she told me he'd been wearing new fawn slacks and a fawn sweater.'

But living ghosts don't only appear at times of death

though there is usually a crisis factor involved. Jim was in his early twenties and living away from home in Plymouth: 'I was studying for my HND in Business Studies and had just finished some course work. I put my feet up for a rest and dropped asleep. I don't know how long I'd been in the Land of Nod but I was shocked awake by a knock on the door.

'I got up from the chair and went to see who it was as I wasn't expecting anyone to call. To my complete surprise my mum was there. She lived in London and I had no idea she was planning to come down.

'She looked so radiant and full of love that I was suddenly overcome with an unconditional love for her — something I had not felt for her for a long time. I threw my arms wide open to greet her, took half a step forwards and she just vaporised there and then. The precise feeling is hard to describe. And I was back in my chair, my head resting awkwardly against my hand. After a moment's confusion, I was opening the door but Mum was nowhere to be seen.'

Jim's experience seems to involve sorting out his feelings towards his mother and enabled him to accept he did still have a bond with her whatever the problems between them. The psychic has an amazing knack of short-cutting or perhaps accelerating psychological processes and a living ghost coming in love can achieve more than 20 therapy sessions.

So if you have got a distant family member you're at odds with (haven't we all?) send a bit of positive love. Who knows? You may materialise with a bunch of red roses in their living room.

In out-of-body experiences the astral traveller is usually invisible. But here Mum was three-dimensional and totally real. It was distress that prompted Cath's appearance to her sister-in law.

Ellen who lives in Lancashire explained: 'We were living in a prefab and my husband had gone in for the early shift. I lay dozing for a while but as I sat up I saw the bedroom door open. In came my sister-in-law Cath. She was carrying a suitcase and she looked awful.

' "How did you get in here, Cath?" I asked. "Sit down, love, you look dreadful. I'll make you a cup of tea."

'But as I got out of bed she disappeared and when I checked the doors they were locked.

'Puzzled I went round to see my mother-in-law in the afternoon. I hadn't seen Cath for ages though we always got on well. ' "How's Cath?" I asked as casually as I could. Mum-in-law looked embarrassed. "She's in hospital with kidney trouble actually," she told me. "She came round here with her case this morning and I took her in. She looked ghastly. I'm quite worried."

' "Why didn't you tell me?" I asked.

' "Cath didn't want anyone to know she was going into hospital," came the reply.

'The strangest thing was I'd seen Cath at the exact time she'd arrived at my mother-in-law's house. Fortunately Cath did recover but I think deep down she had wanted me to know she was ill and was pleased when I went to visit her though I didn't tell her how I'd found out.'

But all living ghosts aren't so well received. Lindsey who lives in Manchester told me of her mum's reactions when her landlord materialised in the middle of the night at the foot of her bed. 'My mum and stepdad were lodging with an old man in Eccles. Mum had the freedom of upstairs since the old man was completely bedridden. But he often used to say, "I wish I could get upstairs again just

111

once more."

'In the middle of the night Mum woke and saw him standing at the foot of her bed. Then he disappeared. She was terrified the old man had died so she told Dad to go downstairs and check on him. When Dad went down his landlord was fast asleep. But we never found out if the old chap knew he'd got his wish, because Mum got out of the house as fast as possible and never returned.'

If this book is full of doom and gloom about deliberately seeking psychic experience then it's achieved its purpose. We all have these abilities and if we cut out unnecessary activity from our lives and learn to listen to our instincts and inner voice then our automatic psychic ability will manifest itself when needed. The danger is, as I said in the premonition chapter, if you're always predicting or flying around astrally when the crunch comes your innate ability can't discriminate between a practice and the real thing.

Remember the international premonition expert who didn't know whether it was safe for her young grandson to travel abroad? To misquote Confucius, 'sparingly, sparingly maketh psychic'.

Chapter Eight

On The Medium Wave

MEDIUMS CAN HAVE a bad press. But when someone we love dies, most of us want to know that he or she is not gone for ever. People who would have crossed the road when passing a Spiritualist church suddenly find that they long for some personal sign of survival. Paul was thirty seven years old when he was killed violently and unexpectedly in India where he was working. His parents were distraught and though they'd never had any contact with Spiritualism went to a medium in London.

Paul's father said: 'We said nothing but the medium waved his hands wildly in the air while he was talking and explained he was being told to do that as a sign and that he could feel great heat and great tragedy. But he assured us the young man who had died was happy now. Paul had always gesticulated wildly when he was excited. Then the medium pointed to Paul's mother's bag and said, "There's something of your son's in there."

'My wife took out a pink tie belonging to Paul and the medium said, "There is a blue tie that goes with it." '

Of course, it could be argued by cynics that it was a fair bet a mother would have something of her dead child's with her and blue ties are commonplace. But Paul's mother had kept the matching pink and blue ties side by side on her dressing table since Paul's death and had, on impulse, put the pink one in her bag just as she was leaving her home that day.

The problem with analysis is that incidents in themselves can often be easily explained away. But it is the unique personal connection at a particular moment that seems to confirm that there is meaning behind what is too often dismissed by those uninvolved as trivia.

Paul's father continued: 'We went to see a second medium soon after who said Paul was talking about an unfinished oval picture with a small one next to it on the wall at home and that he still watched his mother cooking in the kitchen. We do have the picture where he said.

'Paul told the medium I was sitting in the dining room worrying over his affairs which were unfinished. Paul said I must do nothing but wait and it would come right itself. The following week I received all his things from India and all the documents turned up.'

But the story didn't end there because about six months later Paul's granny died and a message came at a spiritualist meeting that Gladys, one of the old lady's names, was caring for a young man with her who passed from the world violently. For Paul's father the contact that began with the mediums is now continued on a personal basis.

'I have been given proof that life is eternal through my son and I know myself when he is near.' It is the apparently trivial personal jokes or memories that make such encounters so believable. Like family conversations in this life the hereafter seems to trundle on in the same way.

I had first hand experience of this when I returned to my home town of Birmingham to interview mediums and clairvoyants at a psychic fair. Inevitably I ended up sampling the wares but I wasn't very impressed with one medium who, having ascertained my mother had died, offered me various titbits that could have applied to anyone. Then she said out of the blue, 'Your mother says do you remember the Burrows family?'

Remember them? They lived two doors down the street when I was a child and son-in-law Georgie's extra marital meanderings provided a welcome addition to the normal over the garden wall gossip, though I got many a clip round the ear for eavesdropping. Yet it was the only thing the medium got right.

I think that we probably have unfair expectations of mediums and if we were prepared to accept that they could get only one clear picture for us, rather than expecting whole scenarios, they would not need to fill in for us or guess. We couldn't then have platform shows where commercial expectations demand a 'good performance'.

Perhaps that's no bad thing and if we recognised that a medium needs financial support, as does a minister of any other religion, then they wouldn't have to put on shows to make a living. Like any other oracle they would speak only when genuinely moved and without pressure. After all we don't expect the average vicar to conjure up an Archangel before we put something on the collection plate. But then, equally, mediums couldn't expect show-biz salaries and this would weed out the fast-buck brigade.

Of course those who communicate from beyond may not send exactly the message we were expecting so it's as well to be fairly open about what you'll get via a medium. There was no doubt at the meeting in Hertfordshire that Grandad was on the hot line. 'I've got a man leading a shire horse,' the medium explained in a bemused manner. I feared for the intricate flower arrangement at the front of the church. Fortunately the lady whom the medium picked was able to stop the horse trampling the displays by enlightening the congregation that her Grandad had been an ostler at one of the breweries and taken care of the dray horses till his retirement.

But Grandad hadn't come back with red roses. 'Tell her to stop all this slimming rubbish. Women should have a proper shape, not look like broom handles.' The woman was not amused. But then elderly relatives aren't noted for their tact in life. So there's no reason a spell in the Elysian fields should have improved their tempers.

At another meeting I attended on the south coast, dear old granny identified herself by a very unusual family brooch down to the initials in seed pearls. 'Was your granny a great one for home cooking?' the medium asked. Here, I thought, was something that must apply to 95 per cent of the pre-Asda generation. But Gran wasn't back with fond memories. 'It's about time you took a leaf from my book,' she scolded. 'All those shop cakes and sliced bread. Cost a fortune and tastes like cardboard!'

It's not only deceased relatives who can bring us down a peg or two from the platform. Friends from childhood get so used to whispering when our petticoat's showing and pointing out our spots that old habits die hard. 'You've got false teeth,' is not a revelation one expects from beyond. I was surprised when I heard it coming from a medium at a small spiritualist group which I attended on the Isle of Wight. But Norma, who was in the audience, realised that it was her late best friend's way of reminding her of a childhood joke.

'Remember how we used to laugh at those false teeth grinning from the glass on Aunty's bedside table when we were young? Comes to us all.' Norma and her best friend apparently used to creep upstairs early morning while aunty was having a wash in the kitchen and muck about with the teeth. Once they got caught and got a good hiding. But it was worth it, Norma told me after the service.

It's often as interesting as the actual clairvoyance to stay after the service for tea and biscuits and to chat to the people who received messages. If a message isn't very personal or does not refer to a tragedy, older people especially may be happy to share titbits from their childhood that help you to piece together the jigsaw of information you've heard. And sometimes you'll meet retired platform mediums or stalwarts of the Spiritualist movement who have a wealth of wisdom and experience to share.

Just as you won't always get the message you expect you may not even get the person you've gone to contact. Bert had gone along to a Spiritualist Church while on holiday in Blackpool because he felt he'd like to contact his late wife as they'd shared many happy holidays in the town. He got a message but it was from an Ernie. 'No,' said Bert quite definitely, 'I don't know an Ernie.'

'Well he knows you,' the medium replied. 'Said you worked in the factory together as lads. You bet him about that pretty girl and he says you lost a day's wages.'

Bert remembered but he wasn't pleased to renew the friendship. 'She wasn't up to much anyway,' he grumbled afterwards. 'We were mucking about making bets who'd ask her out and the gaffer caught us. I got the blame and got fined. Ernie never even said he was sorry.'

Time and time again the proof you demand won't be the proof you get! But then relatives and friends are no more likely to be obliging in the next world than they were here. And it's good to know that somebody's keeping a benign eye on your well-being if it's only the lad who shared the factory bench. But sometimes there is real anger from beyond that can only be assuaged by a public announcement of innocence.

Peggy Peto who lives in Herne Bay recalls how her father came back to clear his name. 'At 9.25pm on 7 June, 1940, my father was killed by a soldier drunkenly driving his lorry back to barracks. My father's right arm and shoulder were smashed and he died of a fractured skull having never regained consciousness. Dad had already had 27 operations on his right arm through osteomylelitis during his lifetime.

'It wasn't until 1am that mum and I returned home to find the police waiting with the news. No one else knew.

'At 5am a neighbour who was a medium called to say, "Edgar has been to me. He wants you to know the accident was not his fault."

'The inquest verdict was accidental death. But my father knew differently.

'Six months later Dad's parents evacuated to Newton Abbot and were tempted to a Spiritualist church. At the end the medium pointed to Grandma and said, "One recently passed over is here. His head is bandaged and his right arm is in a sling and he says, "It wasn't my fault"'.'

The story had a happier ending, although Peggy says the soldier was never brought to justice. 'Two years later Mother was rehearsing the piano at Drury Lane Theatre and in the break she went below stage to the cloakroom.

There were large white tiles along the walls and Mother was completely alone. In one of the tiles was my father in evening clothes and he was quite still but holding his right arm straight above his head. Mother had married Dad in 1916 ánd he had never in that time been able to straighten his arm.'

I am always warning people of the dangers of DIY clairvoyance especially using the ouija board or drawing spirits down into candle flames, a popular alternative to the spirit in the glass. Pauline had met with her psychic group in a bungalow in Wokingham, Berkshire, and they were contacting various spirits with gusto: Edward VIII, a plague victim and even a carpet salesman from the local Co-op. But then a message came through for Pauline. 'It's Father Wallis,' she gasped.

Pauline was a Catholic and Father Wallis had been her parish priest until his death. He had been very anti the psychic and all related matters. And the after-life hadn't changed his opinion. 'Go to church and get on your knees and forget all this dabbling,' was his stern message.

Pauline is still involved in the psychic world but has avoided seances ever since.

So where should you go if you desperately need confirmation that your loved ones are still with you in spirit? Psychic fairs with rows of clairvoyants are not the place to explore personal relationships with the dead, or to gain insights into our hidden psychic life. Ten or more appointments in a day, in an atmosphere where money is changing hands as though it were the first day at the sales, is not, in my opinion, a place to discover anything but the depth of your purse.

I met Petra at an upmarket psychic gathering in London and I could see she was upset. An exotic looking clairvoyant had told the elderly lady that her husband had come through and wanted her to remember the song, *We'll meet Again* that they had loved when he was in the services and that he was giving her red roses. He also wanted Petra to know that he'd never forget her and that he was waiting for her on the other side.

Why was Petra upset? Because she'd met a very nice man at the Over Sixties Club and she now felt she was betraying her husband's memory. So Petra and I went over to the tea bar and had a look at what our bejewelled friend had actually said.

Had hubby materialised between the crystals and incense sticks demanding Petra's total fidelity? Or was the clairvoyant in making a few educated guesses unnecessarily blighting Petra's future? She'd latched on to the fact Petra was a widow — quite likely at that age especially as there wasn't an impatient male in the background tapping his feet.

In fact what the clairvoyant had actually said was, 'You're very lonely,' to which Petra had volunteered, 'I've been on my own since my husband died three years ago'.

But had Petra replied, 'Yes my husband/family don't have any time for me', then we'd be on a different psychic tack. It's unlikely an older woman wandering round a psychic fair alone has got a charabanc-load of close companions.

Another sure fire winner with older clients for a clairvoyant working at half-power and double-speed is a mum in spirit world. If you're awkward and have a mum of 102 who still goes hang-gliding then 'a gran who was like a mother to you in spirit' will fit the bill.

However, the naming of the song, *We'll Meet Again,*

seemed to be the key. Or was it? Petra had agreed with the clairvoyant it was 'their song' — some clairvoyants can get very annoyed if crossed — but when Petra thought about it, that wasn't really their tune at all. *Moonlight and Roses* was, although obviously they'd heard the Vera Lynn song a lot during the war when Reg was in the services. So again, such a choice was an odds-on winner with Petra's age group.

Another hit with hubby being in the forces? Most men of Reg's age were called up. The red roses? Petra smiled. Like the average man, Reg thought flowers were for funerals only. But it might have been that being on the other side had made him more romantic. However, if my research is anything to go by, Reg like most departed spouses would be more likely to come through and say, 'Don't forget to water the flowers', or 'I don't like the new wallpaper'.

But what if Reg was really communicating from the other side? Well he was hardly likely to come through at £20 a throw and say, 'Get on with it, old girl'. And of course, if Petra hadn't met anyone else, she'd have been pleased with the message expressing eternal devotion.

But I have found that departed spouses are remarkably understanding about a new partner. I came across one old lady whose two deceased husbands came through together to chat though they were temporarily miffed when she married number three[1].

But Petra's message just didn't ring true. It was all so general with quite a few misses. I didn't want to be unfair. So we sneaked back to Madame Exotica and hung around a bit admiring the price tags on the crystals.

---

[1]This story is told in *Families are Forever,* published by Aquarian 1993

Once we'd eavesdropped a bit and heard her asking another elderly lady very leading questions and dragging out the red roses and *We'll Meet Again* routine, Petra felt much better.

'Would Reg have minded you getting on with your life?' I asked. Petra thought about it and realised he'd have been glad that she had got someone who'd look after his prize chrysanthemums for him, because the garden had been a bit neglected since his death.

Now if I had wanted to play the medium and had chanced my arm with the observation that Reg wanted the garden watered, I would have been spot on without any astral communication whatsoever. I explained this to Petra and she began to feel much better about life and her new man. Since I haven't had any furious visitations from Reg, accusing me of leading his wife astray, I assume that my non-psychic marriage guidance wasn't too wide of the mark. It's a pity I never heard the end of the story, though.

Of course, we can't entirely blame a clairvoyant or medium if they cut a few corners when the clients are queuing round the block. If we expect to go along to a psychic fair for promises of wealth and instant happiness then a clairvoyant may be tempted to rig the stakes. There's no such thing as a free lunch and often we know only too well the answer to our own questions. But all clairvoyants at psychic gatherings aren't charlatans. I've met caring women who will risk losing a client rather than papering over the cracks.

One such was Zoe who I met at a psychic fair at a steak bar in Wokingham. She'd turned to the psychic after she'd lost her husband and children in a road accident. Her grief had uncovered powers that had been lying dormant since her childhood, when her gran first taught her to read the cards. Zoe was very aware that you couldn't expect a golden future if you hadn't sorted out the past luggage.

'Fairs aren't ideal for consultations but sometimes it's the only time people can come to see a clairvoyant or medium. They can tell the old man they're out shopping and slip in on the way from Tesco and no one's the wiser. After all people could be coming in here for a meal or coffee. Women usually come because they're planning some change in their lives and want to talk it over.

'When married men visit me at fairs, however, they're often having a bit of extra-marital nooky and want permission from the other world. Deep down, however, they're usually worried and guilty. One man came in with his wife and daughter supposedly for a meal and he slipped away to see me. I told him he was having an affair with his secretary at work. He bolted but came back a couple of minutes later when he'd settled them at a table to ask my advice.

'Another woman came with her sister and I picked up straight away they'd got a brother. I kept getting that he was shut out in the cold by the family and this was causing great problems for them all. The women denied it but it came over so strongly I told then I couldn't go on with the reading and offered them their money back.

'At last it came out that their brother had been shut up in a mental hospital and the family couldn't cope with the stigma. The reading gave them a chance to bring the problem out into the open.'

My personal favourite was Jean from Doncaster, a no-nonsense woman who charged businessmen £50 a head and nothing for hard up-pensioners. She used a method she called the kabbalistic runes at a rattling pace with a taped reading thrown in. Every time a bit of excitement

123

came along, she'd told me, she turned off the tape in case hubby played it. In my own reading she promised me a lot of illicit fun with my twin soul. There's an enormous gap in my tape but I'm still waiting.

But all customers at a psychic fair aren't so willing to part with their money. When I went to the Earth Spirit Festival in Birmingham's revamped city centre two lads were arguing outside the door. 'Do you fancy a physics festival then?'

'No, I did technology at school instead.'

At the Prediction Festival in Chelsea Town Hall, two well-heeled middle aged ladies were rifling through the rack of witches' robes and gowns. They were taken with a blue gauzy model edged with sequins.

'You couldn't wear that for walking the dog,' said one.

'No but I could wear it for dinner parties.'

'Wear that? You'd look like a witch!'

If you don't take it all too seriously and avoid paying out a fortune to be told yours, you can have a good day out at a psychic fair, meet some nice people and browse around the stalls. There is, however, no excuse for anyone psychic or otherwise to con money out of distressed folk whether at a fair, by post, phone or in person by promising to get an errant spouse or faithless lover to return — in exchange for money of course.

No one should try to manipulate the mind of a third party psychologically or psychically — and such promises can stop an unhappy man or woman from getting on with their lives. One of the worst cases I came across was that of Pat who is in her late forties. An intelligent, sensitive woman, living in the Home Counties, she almost went out of her mind when her husband walked out after 26 years of marriage for a younger woman leaving her with four children.

Pat, a good Catholic, turned first to her parish priest, who told her that sorrow was 'the burden you have to carry for Jesus and Mary'. From the psychic community Pat got sympathy and compassion but fell prey to more unscrupulous practitioners who made a fortune out of her.

For years she was kept in limbo, paying out for magical forces to bring back her man. Pat tried a postal clairvoyant in Wales — we'll call her Morag, which isn't her real name.

'She charged me £10 per magical working to bring my husband back. She wrote to me: "Dear Pat, I am so sorry for all your problems and thank you for the letter and donation. I am only sorry I have to charge at all but if I didn't I should have to give up my practice and a lot of people would be without healing and help.

' "I feel there is nothing to report except an affirmation that all will be well eventually. I won't stop the working — don't worry about that. Part of what I am doing is to break the hold this woman has on your husband and it is not easy but it can be done.

' "Don't be afraid to confide in me. I have to be discreet and many people tell me their intimate problems."

'A second letter said: "I shall do more occult work at 11-12 midnight tomorrow I feel your husband is going through bad times at the moment and is unhappy. Part of this is because he knows what he has done is wrong."

'A third letter continued: "I am glad you have been able to unburden yourself to me because I am a woman as well as a clairvoyant — never think of doing away with yourself as the day will come when your man needs you again. I will carry on working for you — I am doing another working for you this weekend. It is slow but it will work in the end because changes are coming. I picked up fear and depression and desperation from him in the last working. I feel his time is running out." '

Pat commented: 'Though I paid for several spells, Gavin never came back. Still desperate Pat turned to the alleged power of the talisman. 'I paid £79 for a piece of wood — it was supposedly charged with magic. I got it from Bronwen, [not her real name] another Welsh clairvoyant to whom I wrote after seeing her advert in a psychic magazine. When I wrote to Bronwen she promised that the next spring my husband Gavin would return. She sold me the wooden talisman that would bring him back. At the time I would have paid anything.

'But another clairvoyant had told me my husband Gavin would return the previous spring and he hadn't. I must have spent a fortune on these clairvoyants. I would have sold the house to pay for them. I really mean that. Then I paid £90 for a pottery witchcraft circle from Merlin, a magician from the West Country.'

Pat was impressed, especially as 'I was promised if I bought a talisman my husband would come back. When you're desperate and don't know how you'll cope, you'll do anything. I'd been married 26 years. I'd brought up four children and devoted my life to making a happy home and taking care of my elderly mum. There was no reason to think my world would come to an end.

'Thousands of ordinary women want just that, a husband, children, a home. They work hard keeping everyone else happy. Then it all collapses. Wouldn't you do anything to get your husband back if you loved him and he was your whole life? We shared 26 years. That must have counted for something?

'Then I was offered a gold talisman from a clairvoyant

in south London for £500. I wrote and told him my problem and he guaranteed this talisman would definitely bring my husband back. If I'd had the money, I would have parted with it gladly but I didn't.

'I wrote to clairvoyant after clairvoyant. I couldn't even get out to see them as I had a young son and I had to take a cleaning job though my husband was a wealthy businessman. It was all I was qualified for after those years at home and I had no confidence in myself. When your husband walks out after all those years, you do feel useless.

'They all took my money and promised he'd come back and things would get better but they didn't. But I still went on. I wrote to Olivia, a Midland clairvoyant who was supposed to get the ancient forces to intervene. I bought an ancient piece of stone from her that she promised would change my whole life. It was useless and I even had it analysed. It was a piece of concrete from an unknown source. That piece of concrete cost me £20.

'Was I mad? Yes, with grief and worry about money and the children and no one to talk to and the awful feeling of rejection and these people promised help.

'Looking back on all the readings I had, I think no one can solve your problems or give you the answers. But you need someone to listen to you. There was no one to talk to but clairvoyants and even the bad ones gave me hope till I found they were lying. But it is wicked to make money out of other people's misery.'

As I've said, many clairvoyants aren't frauds and some do a great deal of good to the sad and lonely who have no one to talk to. Some barely scratch a living because they fall for every hard luck story and end up slipping the client a fiver. They are a million miles away from the postal clairvoyants with exotic names and charges to match or the doyens of the upmarket fairs.

The suburban clairvoyants and mediums are on a whole honest, ordinary woman who live at the end of the street or in the flat above and believe that they can help others with their psychic gifts as well as a cup of tea and a shoulder to cry on.

I'm not sure which is the more valuable. I talked to Lilian, a clairvoyant who lives near Bracknell. I first met her when she told me about her psychic childhood[1]. Once again she took me inside her gypsy's tent (or rather her mobile home that now has new estates practically up to the front door). It is here that many of her clients come for tea, sympathy and a bit of good news.

'The psyche comes through the common sense and must be mixed with a firm dose of common sense if it is to help real people in the real world,' she said. 'Many people come to me because they're sad. They've got problems that need sorting out and they're curious to see if I can do what my occupation promises, that is, tell their fortunes, their futures. That is the key. Because their present is unsatisfactory the future is important to them. I get more women than men come to see me.

'About 75 per cent of my customers are women because in spite of women's lib, men are still the doers. Women, ordinary women feel inadequate. Men make them feel inadequate that they don't quite fit the beautiful, successful image of women in the paper or advertising.

'Women today are more isolated within the family. They don't live communal lives supported by other women. They draw the curtains at night and watch television with the immediate family.

---

[1] Her childhood stories can be found in *The Psychic Power of Children*

'Many people who come to me are trying out the psychic for the first time and they get very excited and tell their friends. I get women who work in the local offices and firms, building societies and supermarkets who slip in for a reading in their lunch hour or when they're supposed to be at the dentist and I always give them a tape of the reading. They'll play it to their mates and occasionally mother-in-law or next door neighbour.

'The old man is generally the last to hear about it if at all, because the woman knows he will only scoff. And then their women friends and ma-in-law etcetera, will turn up for a reading themselves. But the old man would complain and say, "If that's what you do with my hard-earned money, I'm obviously giving you too much."

'When a woman comes to see me I'll sit her down and start shuffling the cards. I try to get her to relax and then I ask her to shuffle the cards so her psychic part can get in touch with my psychic part. That's what it's about: getting in touch with people's psyches.

'Sometimes customers want to test me and that's fair enough. They want me to tell them about their past and present and to know what their problems are. They want me to be magic. Sometimes it goes a bit far and they expect me to tell them the colour of their underwear. But basically what they want is very valid. They want me to prove that magic is true.

'I don't find it off-putting to be tested. Why shouldn't they test me when they are investing their hard earned money in me?

'So I give them a reading. I lay the cards out and tell them what is important for them and what will be important over the next nine months. Then they can ask me questions and I can try to help them.

'But as well as my paying clients, I also visit old people to give healing and to talk to them if they are not well. I do the rounds, a sort of psychic district nurse. Most old people have a wealth of experience. It's just they are very lonely, their bodies are failing and they need someone to care. Doctors and other professionals just don't have the time to sit and listen. I'm not blaming them, just saying there aren't the resources.

'Most old people would dearly love to have their experience of life and insights appreciated. Our society wants to cure everything. But with old people, the need is for care, not cure. But it is more than a social service I can give. They may not want their fortunes told — they know they won't have long happy futures, but they want to die peacefully and without fear. I can help them to get in touch with relatives and old friends up there.'

We do expect a lot of both mediums and clairvoyants. Perhaps the whole approach of clairvoyance as a psychic guessing game is wrong and we should regard clairvoyants as especially intuitive people who can help us to get in touch with our own buried intuitions and insights.

If we paid clairvoyants for their time, not for the number of psychic hits they scored, then the temptation to cheat albeit unconsciously would diminish and the real psychic insights on which they built their reputation could shine through.

Best of all we would take charge of our own destinies. In the end, we are our own best clairvoyant for we know ourselves better than anyone. We all have the magic, not as a party trick, or a service to be sold, but as a basic instinct that, if we trust it, will guide us through.

Chapter Nine

Things That Go Bump In The Night

MANY NEGATIVE PSYCHIC experiences occur at a time we are feeling especially vulnerable and may reflect underlying fears and doubts. This is not to say that such experiences are purely psychological. Indeed it may be that our own negative emotions if repressed can open us to dark forces beyond or deep within the human psyche. Carol was pregnant when she had her horrible experience:

'Just before my son was born strange things started to happen in our maisonette in Slough. Doors and windows would open and close. As I lay in bed, I heard a man and woman calling me and someone started to tug at my elbows and wrists. "What do you want?" I asked, but there was no reply.

'It got so bad that I went to the local vicar. He advised me to go away with my husband for the weekend and he would come along to the flat and bless it. After the weekend we came home but things were worse. The blessing seemed to have stirred everything up. One night, while I was in bed a black thing sat on my chest. It was trying to strangle me.

'My husband sat up in bed screaming. It was the first time he had seen anything, for it seemed to be targeting me. I could stand no more so the priest called in a trained exorcist. He carried out a lovely service in the maisonette in which he asked the angel of light to descend and the whole lounge was filled with light. After that there was no more trouble.'

It is the hidden nature of dark feelings, not the actual emotions, that seem to be linked with negative psychic experiences. So it's important in whatever stressful or changing situation we find ourselves to be able to unburden fear or anger without feeling we are wrong to possess such feelings. Negative psychic experiences are usually reported by woman and often seem to occur when they are in bed at night.

Adolescence and the twenties are specially vulnerable times perhaps because it is a period when our identity becomes uncertain and we question everything. I don't believe from the evidence I've gathered that such experiences are sexually linked.

My own theory, and it is just that, is that often women swallow their anger and try to be nice. Even successful businesswomen may on the personal front feel it's wrong to yell. Perhaps this opens some women to negative external forces almost to act out repressed feelings.

Or maybe the answer is simpler — perhaps it is more difficult for men to admit such things as they imply weakness — and, in spite of the 'new man' image, lots of people, some women included, do expect guys to be macho and stiff-upper lipped. I'd be glad of some input from readers on this subject. Sally who lives in Yorkshire also linked her malevolent presence with the unhappiness of the past. She described how she woke one night to find a huge black figure trying to take her over:

'I lay in bed one night expecting to drift off as usual. But I became very alert and felt a figure begin to take shape in a corner of the room. It was very black and very dense, masculine and very malevolent towards me. And it had quite definitely come from me, my middle. It was like a squat little person just standing there and wanting to get back inside me, but I would not let it. At last it went.

'This presence was the way my father had been towards me in my childhood and I always felt my illnesses had resulted from that terrible time of stress. My father had been a very violent man and had died some time before. I knew I had to fight to resist letting the thing back into me.

'Afterwards I was relieved. I had been receiving acupuncture and I felt as though all the bad things and feelings that caused my illness and all my negative emotions towards my father were gone in this manifestation.'

So for Sally the 'black form' experience proved to have a positive side as she felt that it was an exorcism of her own negative childhood. Sylvia, too, had marital problems although she was much older. Her daughter, Joanna, who lives with her mum, in Stirchley in Birmingham, told me the story after I'd given her a free reading at a midland psychic fair.

Joanna's friend had paid out £25 for a short and very unsatisfactory reading from a professional clairvoyant and was disappointed at such a waste of money. Since they were students at a local college I took them round the back and gave them a freebie reading that, without an element of clairvoyance on my part[1], proved more spot-on than Madame Chloe's rip-off. Before we got thrown out by an irate official who felt I was undercutting the professionals, I heard Joanna's story.

'My mum is separated and going through a difficult time. I came in one night to our flat at about half-past ten. Mum is a light sleeper and woke up. We had a chat and went to bed. After a couple of minutes Mum heard people shuffling about her room. Suddenly there was a great weight as if someone had jumped on her bed. Then the whole weight was pressing down on her body and she couldn't move.

'She thought she would be crushed though she could see nothing. Then it was gone. She called to me and as she did so my nan phoned. She'd had the most dreadful feeling something was wrong with Mum and though it was very late, she rang up to check.'

So far nasties in this chapter have all been spontaneous happenings. In each case the malevolence was overcome one way or the other and in some cases may have served as a catalyst for family conflict. More sinister and harder to remove is the malevolence that comes from curses or from dabbling with ouija boards or amateur seances. Untold misery can be caused by hexes. We've all cursed the incompetence or thoughtlessness of others in a mo- ment of fury and five minutes later have forgotten our anger. But some people coldly and deliberately invoke dark powers to manipulate or destroy.

Susan told me the following story in her modern semi in Staines. Though she spoke quietly her voice shook as

---

[1] My do-it-yourself approach to divination without clairvoyance is described in the *Today's Woman* series by Foulsham

she recalled what had happened fifteen years previously when she was in her twenties.

'I had a boyfriend called Bill. He came from a very sad family. His mother lived in the West Indies and his father had been shot in an accident which also left his mother wounded. He never forgave himself for being in London at the time as he felt he could have saved them and his mother never forgave him either.

'Some months later I met a woman called Claire at a party. When she met me she seemed surprised and then told me she had a present for me at home. The next day she gave me two portraits a psychic artist had done at a demonstration in London. Claire hadn't recognised the people at the time but the artist insisted she took them as she would soon find who they belonged to.

'The first was of me, complete with a tiny scar I have on my face. The second was of Bill's mother whom I had met when she came over here before Bill and I were going out seriously. The message with the portraits was: "The older woman will do anything she can to stop the younger woman marrying her son."

'But I reasoned that in view of the family tragedy our relationship was bound to be difficult at first. Besides Bill and I were in no hurry to settle down.

'Not long after I received the pictures, which I didn't mention to Bill, he went to Australia on business for a couple of months stopping en route to visit his mother. He phoned on reaching Australia to say he had got a marvellous cowrie shell that was also a musical instrument. His mother had given him it for me.

'It sounded hopeful if she was sending me presents. He told me that it was so beautiful, he didn't want to wait till he came back for me to have it but it was too delicate to post. Luckily a friend of his who was coming back to England that week would drop it off at my flat in Twickenham.

'I was away when the shell was delivered. On my return I took it in my hands. It wasn't at all pretty like Bill had told me but wide, deep and ugly. I put it to my left ear to listen for the sea and a tendril of black smoke rose. The walls and ceiling seemed to close in on me and a ball of fire rose upwards. Something in me said, "I've got to take it to the water."

'So I threw it into the Thames and it sank without trace. But within days I was in a state of collapse. As soon as I'd blown it I'd known it was voodoo from Bill's mother. But it was too late.

'Eventually, I couldn't stand it any longer and admitted myself to a psychiatric clinic. I never told the psychiatrists about the shell. It was all too improbable and I knew they wouldn't believe me.

'But I was right. Months later a friend of Bill's from the West Indies told me Bill's mother had gone to a woman in one of the outlying villages and paid her a great deal of money to put a curse on me and get rid of me.

'Bill didn't come back or contact me till a year later. When he did return he was like a stranger. He'd been in the West Indies and it seemed his mother controlled him completely in every way. So we split up.

'But I heard he was never happy and eventually he killed himself. His mother died two years ago. I never hated her for what she had done. I felt had we been able to talk we might have even become friends. Or perhaps that is wishful thinking. The idea of voodoo is unacceptable in the Western world but I believe from my own experience it does exist.'

Where the person knows of the curse, then they may fulfil the prophecy of doom unconsciously. And in primitive societies many people do die after the 'eye' is put upon them. Christine, a clairvoyant from Basingstoke whom I met at a psychic fair at a Steak Bar in Wokingham explained that from when she was a little girl she'd put 'the eye' on people who upset her and invariably something bad would happen to them.

'I knew it was wrong but I had a rotten temper and would sometimes feel so powerless it all welled up,' she told me. 'Then when I was 35 I cursed a builder who hadn't turned up when he promised. I was livid because I'd waited in all day. The next day he phoned very agitated to ask if I'd done something to him. He'd seen me jump out in front of his lorry on the M4 as a tyre blew. He'd narrowly avoided a bad accident as he was going at quite a speed.

'Of course I denied all knowledge, but didn't ask why he hadn't turned up. But I couldn't persuade him to come back to fix my house and that was the end of my hexing career.'

Of course, some hexes have a more down-to-earth explanation, not that you can convince the people involved. Granny Burton had a reputation in the 1930s for tea-leaf reading in Ashby and was a formidable old girl on the earthly plane too. So when the tally man diddled her out of sixpence she was livid and tore him off a strip and a half. In his haste to get out he fell down the front steps and broke his nose.

Henceforth, tradesmen were very careful to give Granny B more than her fair measure. They didn't want to end up as toads. And granny never got round to enlightening them that she'd just polished the steps before the tally man arrived.

Usually you know if you've been hexed because you can feel bad feelings hurtling towards you, though not usually as speedily as a recent experience of Alison, from Woking in Surrey.

She was in London for the day and crossing Covent Garden when a gypsy woman asked her to buy some lucky heather. Alison declined politely, but the gypsy was obviously having a bad day, and she muttered something unintelligible as Alison walked away. Said Alison: 'Seconds later a huge force — like a piece of flying steel — hit me.

'Automatically I said, "You can have that back", and I heard the force rebound as if against a wall. As I turned I saw the woman stumble. Was that coincidence? Did I feel hexed because I was feeling guilty for not buying the heather, fear she might curse me?

'On the other hand I've turned gypsies away before and not been turned into a frog. A sense of being the subject of bad vibes is different from anxiety or depression — you can actually feel it as a physical force.'

As Alison says, the real hex-feeling is very rare, so don't panic that ma-in-law has put 'the eye' on you every time you have a disagreement. But if you do feel under attack psychically or psychologically — and it can be very nasty — try to devise a simple private ceremony of protection at the beginning or end of each day. If you're religious, the symbols of your religion and a prayer may help.

If you are not a member of any faith, remember that we can all relate to light and goodness, whether we see it in the form of archangels or as a more abstract idea. You may wish to ask for light and goodness to surround you and even visualise yourself surrounded in light. Drawing fiery pentagrams in the air, or round your house, seems a bit over the top to me, but I have met people who swear that these procedures keep them safe.

So it's really up to you. If these measures do not work, talk to a sympathetic priest. Here you may need to ask around the different faiths or contact a diocesan office to find who is the expert in such matters. Or you may prefer to contact a healing association, or your local Spiritualist Church. The members will help for a donation and are unlikely to charge heavy fees. People in need should not have to pay out for help.

I once was phoned by an old lady who feared she'd been cursed and that some malevolent entity was haunting her home. She'd been asked to pay £100 by a clairvoyant whose name she'd got from a local paper. I put her in touch with the Spiritualist Association who contacted the President of her local Spiritualist Church. He gave her a lot of good advice and as well as sorting out her paranormal problem helped her on a personal level. So don't pay out anything before you have contacted a recognised association. Although I'm sure the healer or medium who helps would appreciate a donation to their organisation or favourite charity.

But by far the majority of nasties come from people who dabble and call up powers from beyond for a bit of fun or out of idle curiosity. And that's where the trouble starts, certainly on a psychological level. And it can end in realms we don't understand.

In Jessica's case, she was a member of a psychic group meeting under the auspices of a well-meaning soul who had read a few books and believed she had great psychic gifts. The sessions sounded harmless enough, taking place in a retirement development in Huddersfield, with the guru's elderly husband banished to the bedroom with a plate of sandwiches and the portable television while spirits monopolised his through lounge.

Jessica told me of the Monday evening sessions where things really happened: 'We were all gifted psychics and the atmosphere was electric. I drifted off and found myself on a boat, a pleasure boat. There was a crash and I fell off the boat and was trapped underneath. I was in the water struggling to breathe.

' "Can you help me out!" I was screaming over and over again. It was dreadful, so real but then the experiences always were at the group and after a while I calmed down. The next morning one of the group phoned me to say, "Did you know the Marchioness pleasure boat went down in the Thames last night?"

'Then the psychic forces began to spill over into Jessica's home life: 'The living room suddenly always seemed dark — you needed the light on even in the day. It was cold too though it was high summer. I could see a man from the nineteenth century or thereabouts. He told me he was a doctor who used to do post mortems to learn more about the human anatomy. He had been executed because he had been accused of killing a girl so he could experiment with the body, but he insisted he was innocent of the murder.

'A psychic friend from the group came along to help me. Phil sat in a chair and the room became freezing. Phil said he picked up the doctor, "but I don't know why he has attached himself to you".

'We both saw him like a transparency and Phil tried to get rid of him. But it didn't work though the doctor did get much less intrusive after that. But it was still creepy and I hated being in the house alone.

140

'Then things started to go wrong in the group as well. One evening I started to meditate as usual and someone walked up behind me and put a hand on my shoulder. I turned thinking it was the group leader but there was no one there. In psychic work the leader had explained that you needed the help and protection of the psychic group and we always set the Archangels watching us so I thought it was safe. I didn't realise that because you'd asked for protection you still couldn't call up all and sundry.

'For a long time I would engage in spirit rescue and feel really good afterwards. It was heady stuff.

'I drifted off again and it felt light and nice. Suddenly there was a hospital bed and an old man lying on the bed. It was so cold. The top half moved off the bed but the bottom part could not move and I was inside the old man. I was trapped between heaven and hell with this old man. When I came back to consciousness in the group I couldn't move my feet. I was so cold. Two of the group placed hands on my shoulders and soon I could move my feet again.

'But the old man would not go. All week I felt shattered. I couldn't let him go. I was cold all the time and I just couldn't get warm. I didn't go to the group for a couple of weeks I felt so ill.

'When I did go, the thought kept running through my head that it isn't only the living who need healing but the dying and the dead. The room was filled with blood and a fellow was coming with a knife. A woman was trying to back off and screaming but no one could hear and she was not able to get away and this brought the most horrendous panic in me, bordering on insanity, a panic beyond belief.

'When I came round, I told the others that a woman was dying traumatically and if you could ask for healing for this world you could ask for healing for the next world. It seemed so important at the time as if I'd discovered a universal truth. When I got home that night I felt totally unreal. I could not get rid of this woman. She was called Mary and I knew I must take her where she belonged.

'She was sitting on my bed so I took her along a corridor with a light at the end. I took her hand. I walked behind her till she was through. She had beside her two gryphons.

'When we got to the gates which were gold, I thought at last I will see what is on the other side. Mary had a baby in a shawl in her arms. The steps shone with light. Suddenly she was gone and I went to sleep.

'Next morning I felt relieved. I sat up and the first thing I saw was Mary's blouse, cotton piquet with leg of mutton sleeves. So I did it all again. But it was no use. I couldn't get rid of her. I felt so rotten for about a week, too ill even to work as Mary was draining my strength. At last I went to an experienced medium and healer I knew and admitted what I'd been doing.

'She told me Mary had walked into my aura. I felt someone pulling a sheet off me like chewing gum and I felt washed and clean. The healer told me that because I was so receptive, psychic entry to me was like a knife going through butter. I had to learn to keep myself within myself and when I felt something approaching to shut off so it didn't enter me.

'I have learned it is very important to protect myself and not just accept every psychic force blindly. That is so dangerous and anyone working in a circle must understand what they are doing and not play with fire. At the moment I just don't want to know about the psychic.'

Earlier, I mentioned the father whose ouija sessions ended up with a malevolent spirit attaching itself to his young daughter. I met Mary at a seaside cafe in Bognor and after we'd been chatting a while the subject veered to the psychic as it inevitably does when people find what I do for a living.

'I'll have none of it,' Mary who is in her sixties told me. 'When I was younger I was into all that. I found by using the ouija my psychic powers really took off. I could amaze my friends and family with my predictions I'd been told by the glass. I even told them all about the Sputnik launch when it was still hush-hush. But then I found I was only getting bad news.

'I was told my best friend's husband was going to die. I asked Jenny if her husband was all right and she said he was fine but I kept urging her to get him to go to the doctor for a check up. Within a few weeks he'd died suddenly of a heart attack. I realised then it was time to stop and I've not touched the board since though still I know things off my own bat.'

Vera wasn't deliberately conjuring up dark spirits but her over-confidence in her psychic abilities caused a certain amount of marital disharmony and could have been quite nasty. She explained: 'I'd been going to psychic classes and fancied myself as a bit of an expert. I was always seeing and predicting things — I suppose it became a bit of a game. Then my husband, Jack, who is very short-sighted was ill in bed for a while. He'd had an operation on his hip and slept in the spare room so he could get comfy.

'About seven o'clock one morning I took in a cup of tea as usual. I thought I could see someone out of the corner of my eye following me but when I looked over my shoulder there was no one. Anyway, there was no one else in the house apart from Jack and myself and the door was

143

still locked. So I was flabbergasted when Jack asked me, "Who's that man who has just come in with you?"

'I laughed and replied, "You don't think that if I'd got a man here, I'd bring him into your bedroom?"

'But Jack insisted there was a man and even described him, whitish hair, pale and slender and wearing a light blue suit. "He keeps trying to attract your attention," Jack insisted.

'But I couldn't see anyone, although all day I felt as if I was being followed and kept catching glimpses of a hazy figure out of the corner of my eye. We called the ghostly intruder Little Boy Blue but I could see my husband wasn't altogether happy about the situation.

'A couple of days later, some friends called. Suddenly I could see Boy Blue in the corner laughing and singing. I started to laugh — he kept doing outrageous things to attract my attention. My friends were scared because they thought I was drunk. Boy Blue was good fun though Jack got even more suspicious when he heard me laughing and no one was supposed to be there. I think I even did a dance and I started singing and my friends left looking embarrassed.

'Next day Ned, a healer friend from Penge, popped by on some pretext. I think my friends had asked him to call though I hadn't told them about Boy Blue. After all I was a bit old for an invisible friend. I was doing the washing up and I wanted to finish. He said suddenly, "You've got a man in blue with you leaning against the sink watching you."

' "I know," I said. I wasn't worried. In fact it was quite flattering I'd seen ghosts before and this one was fun. But the healer warned me little Boy Blue was attached to me and was trying to take me over. I realised that I had been

144

acting oddly with Boy Blue around so we carried out a little ceremony.

'After that Little Boy Blue never came again. But it made me realise that it is important to be careful with psychic powers. I knew I couldn't just ignore my powers but should use them for good not party tricks. So I took up healing and became involved in helping people through the Spiritualist Movement. So some good came out of Boy Blue after all.'

It may sound a contradiction after I have said in a previous chapter that some people see ghosts everywhere and this can be a positive thing. But in Vera's case the ghost was playing games and cutting her off from real-life friends and family. No ghost should take the place of real life contact, even the most loved deceased family member. For we are here to live primarily in this world not the next.

Many ordinary people are convinced we have spirit guides or guardian angels. But real spirit guides do not intrude like Boy Blue and only usually appear in times of need. Mischievous spirits are only a step away from malevolent ones.

But even in the area of the malevolent poltergeist or stroppy spirit all is not doom and gloom. Mary, an experienced clairvoyant and medium, told me how she was called upon to exorcise the poltergeist haunting the upstairs loo of a Middlesex electricity board showroom.

'I was called in by some of the female staff on a strictly confidential basis because every time they went upstairs to the ladies loo this thing would appear and there was more than one case of wet knickers in the haste to vacate the smallest room.

'So one morning while the Manager was out I was

sneaked in. I don't believe in the bell, book and candle routine but had my incense sticks to burn in a nice little ceremony I'd planned. I'd just lit the first stick and was suggesting the spirit might prefer to move on when the smoke alarm sounded. We'd completely forgotten it and the system was wired up to the local fire station only a couple of minutes away. I blew out the joss sticks and tried to hide them in my handbag as half a dozen burly fireman raced upstairs.

'What the shoppers in the High Street must have thought at a scarlet-faced woman sprinting along with a smoking handbag I don't know. But it was a long time before I showed my face in there again. Anyway, with all the commotion, the poltergeist obviously decided enough was enough and never returned.'

Chapter Ten

New Lives For Old

IT SEEMS THAT half the women in south-east Eng
land were once ladies in waiting at the court of Queen
Elizabeth I. Perhaps there is more hype about past lives
than any other subject — and yet we don't know what
information the human brain can access even in the womb
or perhaps carry in our genes.

My research has shown that a large number of young
children do often come up with tantalising hints of past
memories, usually no more than scraps or flashes of
insight. Occasionally adults too recall a sudden sensation,
not just of déjà vu, but of sharing the history of an old
building or area. And usually the link isn't a random one.
This other existence seems to emerge at a particular point
in time to shed light on some current dilemma. At the end
of the day you cannot prove how a person came upon a
past-life memory — we can pick up the most complex and
seemingly irrelevant information without consciously
registering the source.

What is relevant is what past life memories mean to the present lives of ordinary people. Psychology acknowledges that people go on making the same ghastly mistakes time and time again. But if we can trace the original experience, we can sometimes break the pattern. So let's take it just one step further.

Maxine had come to visit me on the Isle of Wight from Wolverhampton and had a lot on her mind. But although Maxine got what for her was proof of a past life, I can't start selling tickets for my regression tour without upsetting someone else's marital apple cart.

We'd gone to a mediaeval manor house with strong Stuart connections and I half suspected Maxine might link into a cavalier or two, since she'd had psychic experiences throughout her life. But she kept returning to a newer section of the house, now part of the museum and sitting on a window seat staring out over the hills. She said out of the blue, 'I'm waiting for someone who went away to the Great War to come back but he's not coming ever and I can't stay here either.'

Maxine told me that she was being sent away because she was pregnant and had no claim on this man's estate as he was a son or nephew of the house and she was only a servant. Her protection had ended when he had gone back after his leave. Now her pregnancy had been discovered by the family and she had to go quickly and secretly.

Then we went walkabout. Maxine insisted on taking me the way she must leave and we ended up nipping through a side path into a tangle of farm buildings that led us eventually towards the churchyard. But the path to the church was covered with nettles. By now I was getting a bit tired and was eyeing up a pub a bit further down the road. But we trekked all the way back and followed the

148

official route to the church and we could see the over-grown gate from the estate was now rusted. Maxine insisted we went to the church because she'd stopped there to pray and that now there was something important she had to find. She knew it was there. With a last lingering look at the pub I followed Maxine down Memory Lane.

Maxine was pretty worried by her present life. Her boyfriend was married and showed very little sign of leaving his wife but insisted that Maxine was his true love. Maxine had always felt very strongly that extra-marital affairs were off-limits. But that was before Cupid shot one of his more dangerous little arrows.

I was probably the worst person to advise Maxine as my sympathies were all with the wronged wife, having been deserted myself years before by a husband who took up jogging with the office bombshell and never returned. But Maxine had decided to stay with me while she worked out whether to give up Charlie.

We walked round the interior of the church a couple of times but she still insisted she was looking for something but she didn't know what. I was heading for the door and the pub when Maxine shrieked: 'I knew it was here!'

On the wall was a plaque to a member of the family who owned the house. He had been killed in the First World War. Most great families lost relatives in the War so I wasn't over-impressed. But she insisted I looked closely.

'Don't you see it's Charlie's name,' she told me. 'I knew the key was here.'

Over a ploughman's lunch I agreed that the first two names had been the same as Charlie's Christian and surname. The chap on the memorial had a pretty unusual name so if it was coincidence it was odds against. Were this a neat story I'd say Maxine realised over the straw-

149

berry gateau she couldn't have Charlie in this life either (my view may be biased).

But Maxine took it to be a sign that she and Charlie were being given a second chance of happiness having been parted by the Great War. And a year on she's still dithering. Psychic therapy can certainly point the way but in the end we must make up our own mind how we interpret the evidence.

In the case of Annie who lives in Bagshot the past life memories were triggered by an outing to a local beauty spot.

'When my hubby and I were courting we went for a walk round Virginia Water. There is a totem pole brought from Canada as a gift for our present Queen. I was amazed as I hadn't known of its existence. I was also surprised by a single line of white light from the totem pole to the woods beyond. Den couldn't see the line and said that the light was playing tricks as it was now dusk.

'So I rubbed my eyes but when I looked it was still there. Den said time was getting on and we'd better get back to the car.

'That was where my problems started. I didn't want to leave the totem pole. Hubby pleaded with me to come home but it took a lot of coaxing and promises to come back because by then I was sobbing. I was so upset but Den kept his word and we visit the totem pole regularly.

'In a series of dream and visions it came to me. In a past existence I had lived in Canada and had three sons. I don't remember my husband. My hair was very black and was plaited past my waist. I hated the settlers because they destroyed our way of life. Our whole tribe was slaughtered, women, babies and children while the men were away. Since going to the Totem pole I've had nightmares about the way we died and wake up screaming.

'I've always found that if I'm upset, I'm happier nearer earth or water and now I understand why. When I have a quiet moment I can recall things from my previous life. Den has promised to take me to Canada to find my tribe but something always prevents us going. Perhaps I'm not meant to go there.'

Annie's past life was uncovered quite spontaneously and unusually doesn't seem linked with any problems in her present world. But by far the majority of people, usually women, probe into past lives through sessions with a regression therapist and find they do link with a present life dilemma. You pay your money and take your choice: an expensive expert in North London or the woman at the end of the street in Bolton or Brixton who has read the expensive expert's latest book serialised in a woman's magazine.

Cynics say that in the first case your regression will depend on which is the current ethnic minority cause in Los Angeles and in the second which B movie was on TV the previous afternoon.

And as one regressionist said to me quite cheerfully: 'If women want to come to me for an afternoon and live out their delusions of grandeur then that's fine so long as they leave their money on the table.'

But she also said it was nice to get people who went back to an ordinary simple existence and took what they needed from it. That convinced her that such experiences were genuine.

Why do so many people — most of them women — flock to be put into trances and re-enact a past glory?

On one level the answer is very simple: many woman do live incredibly dull and stressful lives, juggling part time jobs with families or the demands of ageing parents. And the more unemployment and the recession bite ,the more incentive to get away from the old man snoring in front of the telly and the kids arguing. Isn't half an hour as a Pharaoh's wife or a courtier's lady maiden preferable? And perhaps there's some explanation from way back as to why life now is so rotten. There are more karma experts in Kilburn than Katmandu.

What is more, it may be that a regressionist is unconsciously leading the subject into a particular period. One regressionist's end of term knees-up consisted entirely of former Roman centurions and Indian squaws. Nevertheless, many of the experiences, grandiose or unadorned, are spot on in mirroring present crises. Perhaps the problems of mankind haven't changed that much and in regression we're scooping our bucket into the sea of the collective unconscious much loved by Jung.

But it may be more than that. Perhaps the core of our regression experiences are true. It may simply be that, aided unwittingly or aided by our friendly, trance therapist we are recalling actual incidents from our past but dressing them up into an acceptable form. After all you don't really want to remember picking the nits out of your hair in a straw hovel but there may be some lesson from that time that would be useful right now. So we move the scenario up the road to the nearest castle where we've got maidservants to deal with the nits.

My mother always described my dad who was an ashman as a 'boiler engineer' when we went on holiday, a euphemism that survived all the way to his death certificate.

Take Serena, for example, a career girl of forty living in Manchester who's had a series of relationships but has never settled down. She professes a loathing for children and certainly it is hard to see how they would fit into her almost obsessively elegant lifestyle. But Serena comes from an ordinary background where kids are still regarded as a vital part of any marriage and so there is conflict with her mother who desperately wants grandchildren by her only offspring.

Serena naturally took on a very glamorous past life that she returned to at different times and with different regressionists. She was a Pharaoh's daughter and became a Pharaoh's wife whose greatest sorrow was that she couldn't bear children. I looked up the name of the Pharaoh that Serena had mentioned and the known facts didn't seem to fit with what she had told me.

Could it then be put down to an over-imaginative mind? Or was it an imperfectly recalled name over thousands of years or a half-conscious grasping to find a name to fit a half-remembered but more down-market setting. I think sometimes we can actually falsify experiences by feeling obliged to fit them into known fact. Serena could have been a servant who 'remembered' herself as someone grand.

But the proof is a red herring and we can so easily miss the significance.

The theme continued of the sorrow of childlessness though Serena was still adamant she hated children and despised the subservient female role of this rather pathetic 'other self'.

A happy ending? A clutch of kids for gran? No, but Serena was able for the first time to take on board her softer side, take a chance and throw away her materialistic lifestyle for love. And when it did go wrong she picked herself up and went out and got a really exciting job abroad. However she is still open to the possibility of emotional commitment in the future.

Maureen's experience mixed both formal regression and a spontaneous past life experience on a visit to a stately home. Whether Maureen was nobly connected or a peasant woman living on the estate of the Great Lord who preferred a more elevated scenario, matters less than the fact that her past life gave her the courage to resist bullying from her husband and grown-up sons in her present world. Maureen described her regression like this.

'I was about 27, in a dress so tight I couldn't breathe. I was standing in front of a big window. Then I was at a family gathering presided over by an old man I knew was my father-in-law. My husband had died in France.

' "It's time you got married again and I got you off my hands," he was snarling and I looked next to him at the man sitting there whom I knew had been chosen for me. I looked into the face of a lecher and I hated his weak mouth. My stomach was churning.

' "I can't and I won't marry him," I replied.

' "You will do as you are bidden," the old man said, slamming his fist down.

'As he spoke, I had my hand gripped on the edge of the table and I was rubbing at the edge with my thumb. There was a piece of wood cut out of the groove in a shape like a five-pointed star.

'As I rubbed the wood with my thumb, I was saying over and over again. "I won't do it, I won't."

'Then a tinker came into the courtyard with a tray of pretty things, laces and ribbons. He said to me, "You don't need to buy anything. I'll give you my tiny silver pig. You will need all the luck you can get."

'Eight weeks later. I went to an old manor house near

154

Hungerford with my mum. Things weren't easy at home. My husband knocked me about when he'd had a drink and my grown-up sons treated me like dirt.

' "I've been here before," I said to myself. I knew where the door was and I dragged Mum round to the front of the house. The door was there but there was a notice saying the public weren't allowed to use that entrance.

'I went to another door leading from the courtyard I'd used to go down to see the tinker but that was labelled an exit. I was so confused. At last we found the official way in, a door in the side of the house. But it didn't feel right. That was for the servants.

'But when I went inside it was all so familiar. But there was a tape-recording with sound effects telling the history of the house. It was such an intrusion and I wanted the visitors to go. The Great Hall was set with the big table. I stood at the end.

' "Now where was I sitting?" I thought. I judged where it was and put my hand on the edge of the table and there was the five-pointed star. I walked towards two arches at the end of the hall but there was a barrier in the way. I was shaken rigid. There were ropes wherever I wanted to go.

'Outside was better. It was like being in my own back garden. Mum was surprised when I took her to the river. You couldn't see it from the house. And strangely enough I started to stand up for myself at home and even threw one of my sons out when he threatened me. My marriage broke up but my young daughter and I are very happy.'

At its best past life experience can give us the impetus to break out of an old pattern or as with Maureen, to see some meaning in an unsatisfactory situation. But in the wrong hands — and there are no guarantees that even a hypnotherapist with a recognised qualification can fully control a past life gone wrong — then regression can encourage people to opt out of the present hassle and daydream of former glories.

Countless men died in the Second World War and both men and woman now in their late forties often feel very drawn to the years around their birth. And in regression sessions scenes of being trapped in a burning plane are frequent and sometimes unblock phobias about flying or claustrophobia. So in that sense such memories can serve a purpose.

But Gary, a warehouseman in his late forties, began to accept that knife-edge blend of glamour and terror as preferable to the present existence. Gary's uncle had been a war hero who had been shot down near the end of the war. Gary had always felt especially linked to his uncle as he had been born not long after his uncle's death. His own life was blighted by a sense of guilt and inadequacy and he was only too aware that he didn't live up to the family hero. He felt he had a second rate-job and was bitter about his failed marriage,

In the first regression session he recalled being a boy running round pretending to fly a plane and declaring he was going to fly planes for his country. Over the sessions the story unfolded, his excitement at being trained as a pilot, the thrill and fear of his first raid, his guilt when a school was bombed by mistake and his growing horror as German cities were attacked though he knew retaliation was necessary. He saw friend after friend go on missions and not return.

Finally he recalled being trapped in the burning cockpit of his plane and then, at last, he was at peace.

Gary became convinced early on he was the reincarnation of his uncle and had to be dissuaded from going back to try to trace people from the past, not least his uncle's former girlfriend who was now an elderly lady. And he became addicted to regression and soon found a very learned higher self who would pronounce on the state of the universe.

Of course great insights can come from getting in touch with a higher part of our consciousness but Gary became a sort of spirit super-hero. He was so busy sorting out mankind on a global level that he was actually moving even further away from solving his own, very real problems. At last he broke very suddenly away from his therapist and no more was heard of him or his past life.

Gary did not, to my knowledge, seek out his uncle's — and perhaps his own — former love. But some people do go back and confront past life families, and this can be very risky. For what is a valid experience to us may be a nightmare to others who want the past dead and buried. As with earthly revelations by adopted children and birth parents, for every joyous homecoming are others cases where the past needed a great deal of skilled counselling before it was revealed — and then sometimes could not be resolved.

The whole point is to move on. I don't believe that it is ever a good idea to try to contact a family from a former life. You might succeed only in reopening old wounds. Instead, use the impetus of the experience to make this life more worthwhile.

Sometimes counselling isn't part of the regression process. It may not have been budgeted for. But you can't just give someone an hour, two hours even, stir up a past that may hold potential trauma and leave it at that. I was horrified to discover a regressionist working at a psychic fair.

All forms of psychic work involve tremendous responsibility. Psychological and psychic damage can be done
by an over-enthusiastic amateur or regressionist on an ego
trip and qualifications aren't always proof against the
latter.

For even the best planned regressions can go wrong. No
one can be sure how another person will react to a
regression. I speak from experience. I used to go along to
several psychic groups and sometimes was a bit sceptical
about the number of gypsies and serving wenches among
the regressed executive wives of Wokingham. But then I
hadn't realised that the core of experience was what was
significant. So I decided to try regression out first hand,
both feet first, no checks, no controls, no questions. The
first bit was fine, relaxation, a magic carpet then suddenly
I was on that carpet whizzing through the air at high speed.
I was heading towards the top of a hill. An old woman with
a black-robe was waiting for me. It was so cold and I was
ageing by the second. I cried out, 'My teeth are falling out,
my bones are disintegrating!'

I was later told that the group members were petrified.
The regressionist began trying to bring me back but in the
end I forced myself back. I was shaking and crying.

The strange thing was that all through my life I'd been
plagued by old ladies, starting with a particularly hideous
one who used to drag me upstairs in nightmares as a child.
Then I went through a phase in my teens and twenties
when old ladies would come up to me in the street and start
yelling at me and then disappear into thin air. The final
incident was in the George pub in the Strand in London
when I was 25. My boyfriend was at the bar getting drinks
and I was sitting at a table opposite.

Suddenly an old lady in a fur boa with a grinning fox

head came and sat next to me, abusing and threatening me. As my boyfriend came back she disappeared. He told me he had been watching me from the bar — in those days my perfume was Arpege not eau de washing up liquid — but he had seen no one.

All went quiet on the old lady front until a couple of weeks after the regression. I was driving back from Birmingham towards Oxford after seeing my aunt who was in hospital. I was about to pass the sign to the Rollright Stones on the A34 when I saw the old lady in a black robe sitting in the back seat. I accelerated but kept passing signs to the Stones. There are three or four on that road but I must have passed a dozen or more. It was if I was locked in the same piece of dark road. At last I seemed to get free but not long after a car came towards me on the wrong side. I escaped by putting the car into a hedge and no damage was done.

You can't guarantee a Pharaoh and not a spectre. Dorothy who lives in Bracknell and is in her seventies told me how her first formal regression was her last. 'There was a blackness and a huge bang, nothing in between. I was wearing a suit of armour. My head was pushed back and I was drowning in my own blood.'

Maria too found her first regression wasn't uplifting and seemed totally pointless. 'My eyes were cast down. I didn't want to recognise the pair of sandy feet standing in front of me. They were of a Roman soldier. I identified the crest on his helmet and later checked it in a history book. I went into a village of three or four houses and sat on a rock, eating a funny sort of raw fish. The eyes were like jelly. I wanted to retch but did not dare.

'Then I was on a sea journey. I was in the galley. It was dark and hot and I felt pain and exhaustion and terror that went on and on. Then I was walking through the desert, shackled to the next man. A Bedouin figure on a horse was herding us. I fell face down and I knew I was going to die.

'I rolled over and thought, "Let's get it over with." I was no more than 14 years old.'

I'm not advocating turning our backs on past lives or denying ourselves the support of a psychic counsellor and guide. But we can get spontaneous glimpses when walking or letting our minds roam free. And for some people these are quite enough.

We none of us know whether we recall actual past lives or possess an inner psychic stock cube made from them all. But whether the experiences are psychic, psychological or both, past lives can tell us how to avoid a few of the pit-falls of our present existence.

However, we do need to tread carefully before embracing the personality of a Roman soldier or Tudor princess wholeheartedly. The fact you may have been the wife of a Roman Emperor won't go down well if you're queue-jumping at the check-out in Tesco.

But you may find that some small trace of that former regality might just keep the office creep in his place or trade the last insult in a battle with your teenage daughter. So happy dreaming.

Chapter Eleven

Living The
Psychic Way

HOW HEAVILY POPULATED is psychic suburbia? Hardly anybody lives there or believes in it, you
will find, if you take a quick survey, because few people
will admit immediately to having any belief or experience
of psychic phenomena. They will quickly tell you that this
is territory for the few harmless eccentrics. But if you
relate a few stories, then it is surprising how many people
will suddenly open up and say, 'Ah yes, something, just
like that happened to me — or auntie or a close friend'.

My local DIY shop is a store of hardware and hard-
headed common sense. I was talking to the owner and his
wife about one of my books and Clive was his usual
sceptical self, until his wife mentioned his mum had seen
her mother at the foot of the bed shortly after she had died.
That sent Clive scuttling back to his safe world of paint
and nails. 'It's all very frightening,' he muttered.

It's not really frightening, but there are terrific taboos

around the subject. And if you're not careful you can find that you provoke tremendous hostility and disbelief. Add a bit of earthly nastiness and prejudice and what can start as a psychic quest can end in total tragedy.

I heard sad news about May, a psychic who ran classes for many years in her respectable retirement block in the Home Counties and would organise seances or try to contact troubled spirits who needed help. She is a kind, sympathetic woman who will always lend a fiver or a shoulder to cry on and has helped people who believe that they are possessed. But recently she found herself troubled by a malevolent spirit that she could not get rid of.

His name is Joe and he says he committed suicide after his wife and child escaped to a hostel for battered families. It started as a challenge. May believed that she could help Joe but now he seems to be taking over her every waking thought and filling her mind with dark thoughts and dragging her ever nearer suicide.

Her doctor put her on anti-depressants. She first heard Joe's voice after an injection she was given for depression. Various clairvoyant friends and her psychic group have tried to make Joe go away to no avail. And yet she continued with her psychic classes and insisted that she could help Joe to shed his past.

If the psychic world turns nasty, or you find you're getting obsessed, it's only sense to take up knitting or learn Spanish and to give the paranormal a wide berth for quite a while.

But it was when May's actual world went wrong that the psychic aspect became sinister. May had taken care of her disabled sister-in-law, Christine, on marrying her second husband some years ago. But over the years, May's arthritis had got the better of her and a month ago her elderly sister-in-law had to be admitted to a home. May's husband Alf turned nasty at what he saw as his wife's weakness and started to knock her around.

After he threatened her one night and she was afraid for her life May fled the house in the early hours of the morning and flagged down a police car on the main road.

In her distressed state May was examined by a doctor and mentioned the voices. She got even more upset when she realised the doctor thought she was schizophrenic and ended up in a secure psychiatric unit. However, friends have rallied round and the mental health charity MIND took up her case and provided her with a solicitor. She will get out and her husband who is saying his wife has always been unstable and caused her own injuries will admit the truth.

May had let the psychic world take over so that when her husband turned nasty she was vulnerable to accusations of instability.

Mandy's problem was different. She had never dabbled but she feared her professed paranormal abilities might cause her to lose her children. Mandy, who lives on a council estate in Cardiff with her two children, had some premonitions and wrote to me about them. That was no problem. Lots of people, as this book shows, have psychic experiences and such experiences can be a bonus.

But Mandy read avidly all the psychic articles in popular magazines that she could lay her hands on. And because she was hard-up and lonely and wanted a bit of excitement, she pretended they had all happened to her. Then she told other people about her invented experiences and that's when her troubles started. Out of the blue, some months after our correspondence, I received a very different letter from Mandy.

163

'If I told you I was frightened and I told you the facts could you advise me? I'd been reading a lot of articles in magazines about psychic experiences of floating, reincarnation and an NDE that Toyah Willcox was supposed to have had. I've had a few premonitions I've written to you about before.

'But when a social worker came to see me she annoyed me and I pretended I was incredibly psychic and all the experiences I'd read about were mine.

'It was only a game to shock her. Now she has put me on a medical report and I tried to deny the things but I had to see a psychiatrist. I only said it in jest but I'm at my wits end. I've been trying for ages to put it on paper to you. Perhaps you think I'm mental and won't reply, but I'm not.'

I did reply and tried to get Mandy to talk to someone sympathetic closer to home. She wrote to me several times over a short space of time, afraid her boys would be taken away. Why me? She got my name from an article that appeared in the *Daily Mail* and contacted me through a research agency.

There are few places ordinary people can turn for help on psychic matters where they feel they won't be judged. I suggested that she admitted the truth but told her to insist that she needed practical help with her real housing and money problems.

I put her in touch with a Church organisation that is sympathetic to the psychic and will always help people in distress and a member in Wales did contact her which helped a great deal.

In another letter she told me: 'I feel absolutely terrified. I can't sleep for worrying. I have told the psychiatrist that what I said I made up but he won't believe me. I'll be

164

locked away and I won't see my boys.

'I pay all my bills. I don't owe a penny. I don't smoke or drink. I burn the fish fingers sometimes. I know what I said was pretty silly but they all think I'm mad.

'There seems no one in the world to help me, all these people and organisations. I'm writing this at 3am. I can't sleep for worry.'

I've been on my own with small children and in the hands of money lenders and worried away the midnight hours. So I can understand how afraid Mandy feels. We've all made something daft up at some time based on a kernel of truth, but exaggerated it to make us seem more clever or wealthy or successful.

But the psychic world is still a no-go area with many people, so it's important to accept that psychic instincts are quite natural and common but shouldn't ever be sensationalised or exploited.

Putting it cynically, if you are wealthy and powerful, it's fine to see ghosts in the ancestral pile, or even in your converted attic in your four-storey town house in Islington. But if you're a single parent and dependent on help from the social services, it's as well to be pretty careful whom you tell about your psychic experiences.

President Mitterand of France might have given his backing to a campaign by Elizabeth Tessier, one of France's leading astrologers, to reinstate the study of Astrology at the Sorbonne; Ronald Reagan may have been influenced by an astrologer while he was president of the United States, according to some sources; and the study of astrology may have a strong tradition in Asian politics. But if you are in the suburbs, then pushing the psychic can mean pushing your luck.

However, the psychic does fulfil a human need in an

age where few people turn to religion and family units are too often scattered wide. Genuine psychics are usually very warm, sympathetic people who aren't concerned with making a fast buck and do provide a listening ear.

Barbara who runs a magic shop in Reading explained: 'Countless people just pop in to talk. Where else can they go? They can't start pouring out their hearts to the girl behind the till in Marks and Spencers.'

Brian and his wife Jean have the largest psychic mail order business in Britain but still run a shop in Ashby de la Zouche (as well as one in Brighton) and attend all the major psychic fairs. Being a Midlander like them, I'm obviously biased in their favour. But I believe it is true that Brian, a skilled trance medium, and Jean embody the compassion and common sense that gives the psychic world its good name without the witchey-poo elements. Brian explained his own entry to the psychic shopping market:

'Originally we sold our home in the Midlands to set up a psychic shop in the wilds of Wales. I'd always been interested in the psychic and we got the idea on holiday. I supposed I imagined days sitting on the beach and trips to the mountains. But it really took off and what with the shop and the shows we never saw the mountains.

'Mind you, for starters we fell foul of the local tourist board almost at once who warned visitors we were the sort to sacrifice lambs on the hillside.'

'The only lamb we had was for Sunday dinner,' Jean commented.

'Because we were so busy,' said Brian, 'we never had time for sunbathing or sightseeing so we decided we might as well go back to the Midlands. We settled this time in Ashby, at the centre of the Midland motorway network.

166

'However, even here it wasn't all roses at first. We hadn't long been open when a local TV station sent in an investigative team, hot in pursuit of satanism. They got pretty bored watching little old ladies come in and buy pot pourri.

'People take ages to pluck up courage to come in and then say, "Oh, but it's normal". They'll come in for candles and find it's OK and they're not going to be turned into a black cat. They go out with a book they've bought and usually come back.

'People can get very worried about the psychic. When we were in Wales, one woman locked herself in the car while her son and daughter-in-law came in to the shop. But magical practices is not what it's about. On an everyday level I am involved with people's problems. I am a trance medium and my spirit guides do speak through me to help people.

'But what people need most of all is someone to talk to. People come in for Tarot packs and the like and I deliver them a lecture.

'The Tarot can't solve your problems. It's only people who can change. The local kids go to these video parties and come in here wanting the witchey bits without a clue what to do with them.

'Sixth formers are into ouija boards — they think it's clever. But I'll only sell them to adults and then with a stiff lecture about the dangers of playing with what you don't understand. The psychic world isn't a game.

'In the Midlands,' Brian concluded firmly, 'we like to keep things very low key.'

The same goes for Hereford, where, as I write, a controversy has just blown up over women priests who celebrated their ordination by circle dancing. They have been accused by some Christians of dabbling with witch-craft.

The Bishop of Hereford, the Right Reverend John Oliver, who took part in the dancing while wearing his robes and mitre, said it had nothing to do with witchcraft or the New Age.

He did, however, admit to feeling somewhat self-conscious as the women linked hands and took a succession of steps to the front, back and sides and sang a chant based on the psalms. One of the dancers, the Reverend Janice Fox, said the dance was a form of prayer. 'It was very slow and meditative,' she was quoted by newspapers as saying. 'We certainly didn't think we were doing anything controversial.'

I am not suggesting for a moment that the women priests were doing anything out of limits to any Christian. I, myself, have been circle dancing in a church hall outside Wokingham that was supposedly sited where two ley lines cross. I was introduced to the craft by an electrician called Hugh who promised me a very spiritual experience.

However, since I kept getting the steps wrong, the spiritual side of the experience was somewhat diluted by the snooty comments from some of the more practised members of the group. I felt that rather than a deeply spiritual or psychic experience it was more like trying to make your way with the local Come Dancing fanatics.

But in view of the hostility that the dancing women priests seemed to have summoned up — if nothing else — I would recommend that they take Brian's advice and keep it all very low key. What does not seem controversial to you may seem like sheer devilry to your neighbour, so watch your step.

And that is pretty good advice generally if you step into

psychic suburbia. It's certainly not all black and white. Loneliness is the scourge of the modern age and sometimes a spirit presence is seen as better company than no one. Far-fetched? Then maybe you've never stood hour after hour at the window watching for someone to come home, or, worse still, known no one is going to disturb yet another evening of nothing but the television.

Or perhaps you have never walked alone on a drizzly Sunday with a small child in a single buggy while the world is full of happy families. I can understand the problems of Lucy who lives as a single parent in St Albans with a small child. She wrote to me initially because she had felt a spirit touching her. Then she saw a ghost in the night, an old woman who sat with her and her baby when he was ill.

During our correspondence, she told me about her lonely hard life. Having been a single parent I remembered the experience all too well. I put her in touch with the members of a helpful religious organisation I knew of, who would actually go to see her and give her personal contact without demanding money or insisting that she joined them. After that, Lucy and I lost touch.

A couple of years later, quite by chance, I was telephoned by the person she'd told me was helping her. He wanted me to give a lecture to his organisation and I was able to hear how Lucy was. After a lot of help, Lucy had come to the conclusion that she actually relied on her benign spirit, especially since her earthly life was dogged by depression and difficulty.

At one point she tried to commit suicide, not because she was 'possessed' but because her life seemed without hope. This serves as a sharp reminder that it is no good any of us offering help, whether through clairvoyance or counselling, if we can't keep it up as long as the person needs support, which may be for years. Answering a psychic problem or busting a ghost may be high profile. But the psychic element is only one factor and we can stir up all kinds of emotional and practical traumas if the psychic issues aren't followed through on the material front.

Many people do believe they can load the dice of life by casting spells. One respectable lady in the Berkshire suburbs does a rain spell so it won't rain when her boyfriend fixes her car, while another has a chant for when she puts her washing out.

But few would go as far as one woman to ensure her husband's success. On July 4, 1993, it was reported in the Independent on Sunday newspaper that the night before the European Cup, Genevieve Boli, wife of champion footballer Basile Boli sacrificed a lizard at her home in Marseilles. 'I did as I would have done in my native Senegal,' said Genevieve. 'It was for Basile to bring him luck.'

The offering seemed to work. A few seconds before halt-time in Munich's Olympic stadium, Basile Boli scored. His goal had won the European cup for Olympique de Marseille.

But Mme Boli's spell didn't last. On July 1, five weeks to the day after her husband had woken from his night of celebration, he was taken away to be questioned by the police along with 11 of his club mates over allegations of bribery and match-fixing.

Perhaps Genevieve should have stuck to the traditional British eye of newt, or tried a commercial potion. Spells are big business. Go to any psychic fair and there will be a stall of strange packets of herbs with exotic labels and price tags to match promising love, happiness and wealth.

Ask the name of a psychic profession and most people will answer 'medium'. But you could answer 'nursing' or 'social work' and be equally right. It seems that some professions make people especially receptive to the psychic. Or perhaps the natural sympathy for others that draws a person to the caring professions mirrors the qualities needed for our psychic radar to be switched on. Certainly I've come across dozens of psychic nurses, midwives and health visitors.

In one suburban surgery I attended some years ago there was a psychic midwife, a psychic health visitor and psychic practice manager. The receptionist was also psychic but kept it under wraps. Penny the psychic midwife was an expert animal healer and the other staff would bring in their sick pets after surgery for Penny to sort out. An elderly senior doctor was heard to complain one day: 'It's more like a ruddy vet's than a Health Centre.'

However it was a different story when his old back injury started playing him up. 'I don't believe in all this rubbish,' he grumbled to Penny, 'but you might as well have a go at my back.'

I'd like to report that the cure resulted in a Road to Damascus conversion and alternative practices all round. But the doctor put the improvement down to auto-suggestion and still dishes out pills like smarties.

Penny told me about some of her psychic nursing experiences: 'I went to work in an old people's home. On my first morning, I was asked if I minded laying out an old lady who had died early in the morning. The next day, I was doing the breakfasts when an old lady walked into the kitchen wearing a beautiful Mediterranean blue flowery dress. I smiled and she smiled back.

171

'She was as real as you are,' Penny explained as we sat in her modern south London maisonette while her teenage daughter crashed round us.

'Then I thought, "It can't be. It's the lady I laid out yesterday". I put it down to my imagination. Two days later, the woman's daughter came over from Canada. The Matron asked me if I would give the daughter the key to the wardrobe where she had put the old lady's things and stay with her in case she was upset. As she took out the clothes there was the blue flowery dress.

' "That was mum's favourite," she told me.

'A couple of days later I was doing the coffee round. The room on the end of the top landing was open and empty, but I glanced in automatically. There was a very old lady sitting up in bed wearing the most beautiful cashmere cardigan.

' "Well I'm blowed," I said, annoyed because I was late and would have to go downstairs for an extra cup. "They might have told me a new resident came in last night."

'So I went back to the trolley and poured her coffee. When I got to the room again the old lady was gone. I finished off the coffees and went downstairs. I asked the matron about the old lady in the end room.

' "Oh that was old Emma's room. She loved it. She died not long before you came. She always wore the most beautiful cashmere cardigans."

'When I was on the district all sorts of funny things happened to me. Once, in an old house in Wandsworth, two children in Victorian dress shot past me on the landing chattering and carrying books under their arms. It wasn't till they had gone past I realised their clothes were strange but I reasoned they must be going to a fancy dress party.

'I mentioned this to the new mother and she laughed,

"When my husband sits on the settee, the children bounce on either side of him. I can feel them though I can't see them but he often does. In fact, they're a regular fixture round the house."

'One Easter I went to see a mum and new baby in a house in the same area. Mum was upstairs and the baby in the conservatory.

'I went to fetch my nursing notes, shut the door and sat down in the conservatory to read them. The door opened and in came a girl in mid-seventeenth century dress of a deep blue cotton material, She had a straw hat in her hand and lovely long dark hair worn loose. And then I saw a figure lying on the floor, a thick set man with a blood red face. I realised he had had a stroke and automatically I dashed over to help him. But how can you treat a patient who isn't there?

'The girl screamed and ran out. I went back the next day and saw nothing till I reached the door on the way out. There was a crowd outside. The servants had their pinnies over their heads crying their eyes out. The girl was wearing black and getting into a light carriage and I knew she was going away forever in appalling circumstances. I walked through the crowd and they were gone.

'In another house, where the family had lived for generations, I looked in a Regency mirror as I walked upstairs. I saw a flash of a lady with an emerald green long dress and frizzy hair. She had a brooch with the name Christina written in pearls.

'As I was chatting to the mum — it wasn't one of my cases so I hadn't even a chance to read the notes — I asked what she'd called her baby.

' She said: "Christina, it's a name that's been in my husband's family for years." '

Penny found that, whether she was visiting an old house or a new block of flats, she was linked to the past. So if your district nurse or midwife starts looking over her shoulder, ask her what she can see.

It's not only professionals who live the psychic way. Janet is a housewife living on a new estate in urban Berkshire. She is a single parent with two young children and, like many women who are attracted to the psychic, belongs to a psychic development group that meets in someone's front room each week. Janet explained how she got involved:

'My gran used to read the tea leaves and the playing cards when I was a child living in Bury. I grew up accepting the psychic as a natural part of life and it wasn't till I went to school I realised other people were different. I always saw things and heard things.

'My mum and dad were very anti-psychic. Gran and I were the weird ones in the family and when Gran died I was alone. I'd started to go to Spiritualist Church to meet people who were like me. My boyfriend's mum was a Spiritualist and it was like coming home. But when my mum found out she went up the wall and stopped me going as she said it was too dangerous. So I started doing the tea leaves and got my first Tarot pack on the quiet.

'When I got married it all died down. I was trying to be a good wife and mother and please my husband and he wasn't interested in anything outside his own narrow world. It wasn't till we separated that things really took off psychically. I met another girl with a broken marriage at the local spiritualist church and we decided to join a psychic development group so we could do magic as well. We saw one advertised in the paper.

'We started going to Candlemagic sessions held by the

174

group leader on the new moon in her maisonette in Bracknell. You light candles of different colours according to your birth stone and what you want and ask the Archangels to help. We put our jewellery and money in the centre to attract wealth though the leader says you should first ask for health and just enough money for your needs. If you get that, she says and still aren't happy it's no use blaming magic.

'Afterwards we have sandwiches, cakes and trifle to earth ourselves. I always seemed to get my petition answered, but I do wishes myself as well. I suppose you'd call them spells. They work and are an important way I deal with my life.

'The group really opened me up in a psychic way and is a central part of my life — I've met lots of people just like myself and have made so many friends, not easy as a single parent. I do Tarot readings, tea leaves, psychometry, runes, I'll try anything and am in close touch with my guides, a Red Indian, an African and Arab who help me in my work. When we do sessions with the group I can sometimes feel myself change into a Red Indian girl — go all itchy and feel strange. I constantly feel the spirits close to me when we are doing our psychic work but I won't let them inside me.

'But I do most of my psychic work at home. I can't do paid work because the children are so young. I always use Darjeeling tea for readings — it gives a clearer picture. I hope to turn professional before long and that will ease my financial worries a bit. When I'm doing readings or looking into the candle I see visions. The magic is always there but I wouldn't use my powers to get money for myself or an attractive new man, tempting though that would be.

175

'I believe my psychic gifts are meant to help others. I'll often help people who are troubled with ghosts. My friend Sarah, for example, had a really creepy presence in her house and so I cleansed her home using water I had left standing outside my back door in a bucket for 24 hours to be purified by the sunlight. I keep a supply of specially prepared water for occasions like this. At Sarah's house I also used salt and blessed the four corners and I took along my pentacle, though you can just visualise this if you haven't got a real one.

'I felt the presence leave. I hadn't asked it to go because if it was a spirit of light it would be handy to have around. Besides you don't want to throw out all your old relatives who hover around to protect you. I've got my late Dad, mum and gran who all pop in to see me and my gran comes through in automatic writing — I change into her tiny spidery script. She just chats about ordinary things and always sends her love in the messages.

'It's hard work sorting out spirit problems. I starve myself for 12 hours before, don't smoke which is difficult for me and I drink only water. Then I have a bath just before I go to cleanse myself. I take four candles to light for the four main Archangels as it's important to get protection at the four corners of the house before you start.

'The psychic is an essential part of my life now. I couldn't live without it. Lots of women do lose their magical side when they marry and have kids. I suppose it's inevitable but if I married again my new partner would have to understand my psychic work and fit in with it.'

Janet is a sensible, intelligent woman and yet she thinks it's important to consult her cards or leaves before making any major decisions. And she's not alone. Lots of people do have this hidden magical world coexisting with their

176

outer lives. Is it a compensation for loneliness or a search for meaning and permanence in modern society? Is it healthier to pursue the psychic path rather than drowning our unhappiness by watching soap operas on TV.

I spoke to a psychologist who asked not to be named since she was commenting on cases she'd never met. 'Women like Janet are compensating for inadequate lives by substituting a fantasy world in which they are all powerful and can control their future, whereas they can't do much about their actual social or economic position. But it can be dangerous if they opt out of the real world and gradually substitute their fantasy existence.'

I'd agree as I said earlier in the chapter about the dangers of amateur ghost-busting and exorcisms. It can be disturbing on many levels. But my psychologist friend could offer no real alternatives for Janet and other women struggling with financial troubles and problems of loneliness.

'Perhaps counselling would help such women to come to terms with their situation. But then such resources on the National Health Service are scarce and can't change the reality of the situation only the women's perception of it,' she said.

Which is what magic does. Of course the psychic way may be no better. But until we can offer single parents and other lonely people real support, make sure everyone has a decent home and enough money for their needs, and provide the next generation with open places to play, a good education and the prospect of full employment, then we can't offer a lot more than magic solutions using conventional therapies.

This book ends as it began, by saying that when a psychic experience occurs naturally, don't be afraid to use your innate powers of telepathy, premonition and that ability to see and travel to other dimensions which you last enjoyed as a child.

But remember everything has a price and there are no free lunches or rides in magic or in life. So if you're lucky enough to have a magical experience value it. Realise that there is more than this world that at times can bring more sorrow than joy, and that life may well go on beyond the grave in an everyday way. We may even recreate our Acacia Avenue in the sky — some might prefer it to a marble hall without wall to wall carpeting.

But once you've had your magical lift, you have got to apply the impetus you have gained to the daily round of hard slog. You will probably not have a career as the next Doris Stokes — and even she found that, once she had become famous, the pressures on her to deliver the psychic goods were overwhelming.

It is also important to remember that magic cannot bring you everything — and can sometimes bring you the wrong thing, as I found out when I asked Lilian, the Bracknell clairvoyant, about people who asked her to do spells on their behalf.

She told me: 'Spells are usually to do with love affairs, to feel desirable or to stop a partner straying. It's mainly woman who come to me for help to load the dice in their favour because ordinary women often feel inadequate.'

'But do spells work?' I asked her.

'If a person really wants a spell to work then it will. I think that part of the secret is that when you have had a spell cast, then you change yourself unconsciously to achieve your goal.

'But on a psychic level you can get things going and project your energies to achieve that leap. And that's where the ritual is important as well as the actual magical herbal or other ingredients you might use.

'When you are performing a ritual, you are spelling our your intention — literally — and your physical ritual translates into mental and psychic action. Our inside world gets in touch with the energies out there that can move mountains — or at least help you to keep the old man on the straight and narrow, if that's what you really want. Few people, especially women are interested in getting instant money, it's love and being loved all the way with them.'

'So it's all plain sailing?' I asked.

'Not quite. Sometimes people will expect me to wave a magic wand and — hey presto! — the man of their dreams will be waiting in Bracknell High Street. After the spell you've got to make an effort, not sit and wait for your prince to knock the door. Spells are the first part. But occasionally you'll get someone who thinks that, once you've had your fling or nooky or wine and roses, you can return the guy or gal like a library book.'

'What do you mean?' I asked imagining a nearly-new sale of discarded lovers.

'Take one client I had. Janet really fancied this guy who lived in the next street. So we did the spell. Then we made a talisman made out of tiny hawthorn twigs and possets of dried flowers to put under her pillow. But two weeks later she was back with a face like a fiddle.

' "Didn't the spell work?" I asked.

' "Too well. The guy is crazy about me. The trouble is that when I got close up to him I realised I didn't fancy him at all. I prefer his friend who'd asked me out in the first place. Can you get rid of the first guy? He's getting on my nerves." '

Even if you decide not to have any truck with deliberate magic-making, then you will probably have, at some time, a psychic experience whether a predictive dream, telepathy with someone close, a sense of being protected or a full blown visitation.

Ordinary people like you and me, not just the nobility, the incredibly rich or academically qualified, are magical and special and will see our visions, not on a remote mountain or in a research laboratory, but in our own front room or waiting at the bus stop.

Look at a little child asleep, however awful he or she has been during the day. Watch the sun rise fresh and new over the scruffiest piece of wasteland and believe that however dreadful and depressing yesterday was, today, perhaps will be different.

Magic is all round us and most of all within us whether we live in a terraced street or tree-lined boulevard, a remote village bombarded by the forces of nature or on the twelfth floor of Canada Tower in London's Docklands. Forget for a moment the overdraft, the dripping washing and the car that's failed its MoT for the fourth time. They'll still be waiting — we're talking about magic not miracles. Cast your unique spell on psychic suburbia right now.

It is of course very easy to get above yourself on a psychic ego trip. As I have said, I am often contacted by people in trouble because of some form of psychic phenomena. Recently I arrived home one evening from a picnic with my younger children to find half a message on my answering machine. My older two offspring have a habit of chewing up my messages while searching the answering machine for the endless stream of messages that enhance their social whirl.

An old lady's voice which I did not recognise pleaded: 'Please help me I need your help urgently. Contact me as soon as you can.'

What was wrong? Had she seen a ghost? Was a poltergeist smashing her china? Was something from the Dark World trying to possess her?

She gave an address which I tracked down through my address book and full of ghost-busting zeal I rang her and asked: 'How can I help you? I telephoned as soon as I came in.'

'I've got a callous between two of my toes and I can't walk properly. You've got to help me!'

She'd wanted a chiropodist but had dialled the wrong number.

If you have enjoyed this book you will enjoy

The Psychic Power of Children

Cassandra Eason's study of the paranormal abilities of ordinary children began after her two-and-a-half-year-old son 'saw' his father having a motorcycle accident 40 miles away. After talking to other mothers, she realised that such incidents were neither uncommon nor anything to be afraid of.

The book, re-issued by Foulsham, with many new cases, looks at telepathy, prediction, invisible friends and phantom foes, and the ghosts of children. It deals with a delicate subject in a sensitive manner which is also down-to-earth and humorous.

Cassandra Eason is also the author of the

Today's Woman
Divination series

Each is written in the same easy-to-follow style and, in a six-week course, concentrates on developing your powers of intuition rather than relying on expensive clairvoyants to choose your path for you.

Once you have learned one system, it is very easy to move on to the other forms of divination described in these books.

Rune Divination for Today's Woman

Many women don't use the runes for divination because, at first sight, they seem so complicated. But you do not have to be a Viking or a professor of Old Norse to tap your own hidden powers.

Step by step, this book shows you how, by drawing simple symbols on pebbles, you can tap into a magic that is as fresh today as when Nordic and Anglo-Saxon women first tried to juggle relationships and family with the need for finding their own identities.

Pendulum Divination for Today's Woman

Whether your pendulum is finest crystal or an old key on a piece of string, you can use it to dowse, not for oil or water, but for your future options and your present health. The system uses simple circle cloths to focus your natural intuitive wisdom and ensure that you stay in control of your own decision making.

There are also sections on finding lost objects, dowsing for health and even — for the more adventuruous —dowsing for ghosts.

Tarot Divination
for Today's Woman

At first sight, the ancient symbols of the Tarot cards appear to have nothing to do with modern life. But they can easily be adapted to the lives of women today, using a very simple spread to build up a picture of the options which life is making available to you.

For this is fortune-making, not fortune-telling and relies, not on some external magic, but on your own very powerful intuitions.

Crystal Divination for Today's Woman

Crystals and semi-precious stones provide a very powerful form of divination by harnessing the energies of your own powerful inner magic.

You don't need to be the fabulously wealthy owner of a vast collection of gems nor an expert geologist to use the system. It is a simple — and cheap — system which is based on a very simple colour method which you can adapt to your own special needs.

I Ching Divination
for Today's Woman

Take away the image of the male Chinese civil servant which until now has dominated the I Ching and it reflects a woman's natural approach to magic and change. Using the more ancient system, based on the natural forces of fire, sky, water, earth, trees, thunder, mountains and lakes, women can interpret their own present and plan the future. The book shows how to make simple I Ching pebbles to work out your trigrams in seconds.

Moon Divination for Today's Woman

Moon Divination puts women in touch with their natural inner cycles that, from the beginning of time, have been linked with the phases of the Moon. It uses Planet Stones made from ordinary materials and a Moon Cloth to harness the power of our inner astrology. But the book is not about worshipping a Moon Goddess. It deals with the everyday problems of modern women.

About the
Author

Cassandra Eason is a mother of five children and lives on the Isle of Wight. She juggles writing and broadcasting with taking care of the family, and the vacuum cleaner with the word processor, and frequently ends up fusing both. From an ordinary home in the back streets of Birmingham, she won a scholarship to an exclusive school (her Dad's bike would be parked alongside the Rolls-Royces at Open Evenings).

She became a teacher and then married a nice middle-class boy but found out that nice china at tea-time wasn't the same as a warm heart. They split up and Cassandra was rescued from a tumbledown cottage in Cornwall with two small children by a middle-aged knight in a Renault 4 whom she later married. Together they had three more children.

While the children were small, Cassandra trained took a degree in psychology with the idea of returning to teaching once the youngsters took up a little less of her time. But she was pushed into a writing career when her middle son, Jack, told her casually over breakfast that his dad was falling off his motor bike as it was happening 40 miles away.

The response from ordinary mothers to whom she related this experience led to her first book, *The Psychic Power of Children,* which looks at the extraordinary psychic experiences of ordinary people, rather than concentrating on the tales of famous haunted castles and the phantoms of the gentry. This book has now been re-published, in a revised version with many new cases, by Foulsham.

Cassandra's interest in divination methods, such as the Tarot and the Runes, began while she was researching *The Psychic Power of Children* and *Psychic Suburbia.*

Since the publication of the *Today's Woman* series, she has appeared on radio and television demonstrating her methods of fortune-making rather than fortune telling.

Cassandra is always pleased to hear from readers and tries to answer all letters. She can be contacted through her publishers.